Althar Intense
The Unconscious

Joachim Wolffram

Also available from Joachim Wolffram:
"Althar Intense – Space, Time, Veiling"
"For You – Records from Your Lives"
"The Free Human"

The Althar series:
Volume 1: "Althar – The Crystal Dragon"
Volume 2: "Althar – The New Magi"
Volume 3: "Althar – Towards Utopia"
Volume 4: "Althar – The Final Letting Go"
Volume 5: "Althar – Opus Magnum"

**For information about audio recordings
and workshops please visit:**
www.wolffram.de
or
facebook.com/joachim.wolffram

Contents

Preface

The following text is a transcript of the live messages Althar and Aouwa gave at a workshop in Karlsruhe, Germany, in September 2019. In some places, the grammar or sentence structure has been corrected and occasionally some words have been changed or added to make a statement clearer.

As a transcript cannot adequately reflect the actual dynamics and atmosphere during the sessions, the audio recordings of this event can be purchased at www.wolffram.de. These are specifically helpful for diving into the guided meditations and the light body exercise.

Snippets of the audio recordings are available here: wolffram.de/ai-the-unconscious

*

I would like to express my heartfelt gratitude to Nazar Fedunkiv for creating the initial transcript and to Nina Spitzer for editing the final version.

Thanks to both of you!

1. Introduction – End of Preparation – Uru – Enlightenment in the Now – True Encounter

(Music "Waiting for the End", from *Lincon Park*)

I am Althar, the Crystal Dragon!

I welcome you, dear friends, and friends you are. Even though many of you meet just for the first time in the physical reality, we've all known each other for a long, long time.

This specific gathering has been dreamed of literally for eons. There were eons of preparation and nobody knew the outcome of all those preparations. Nobody knew. Nobody knew who would finally arrive here at this spot. Some heard the call, others heard the call and decided not to come or to stay in what I call an outer ring. It's very interesting how prior to such an event people who signed up suddenly break their ribs, break their cars, break anything to find a reason not to come. But this is not a real problem, because those who are here in the physical are enough to create a critical mass. And then there are so many who participate in human form from the outer rings. They are in their home country, they know what we are doing, they know that we're heading to and they connect with us right now, they are here just as well. They've been even in the preparations for this gathering, for something like this – an event like this – doesn't take place only in the physical like that. No, there's lots of tests and tries, and we checked what would work best to really... how can we say, *celebrate* this gathering. For a celebration it is. You reached a critical point that I call a *milestone*, a true, true milestone.

In the opening, some of you said that you might not have read all the books even though you skimmed through them. Well, that doesn't matter too much, for you know the content anyway. Here, we will bring all the wisdom that's in the books into experience.

Even though you might not have explicitly read about it, you might have heard about the fact that the incarnation required very drastic measures by a group called Uru, who compressed you and hypnotized you so that you finally came to believe: "I am a physical body." Being able to incarnate was a major milestone in all the attempts for embodied ascension. But as difficult as it was to bring consciousness and matter together, it is *as* difficult to release them from each other. For all the drastic measures that were taken left an imprint on you. They have created a big fear and shame and many things that you have to face if you want to let go of the physical and become the true embodied master that you wish to be.

So, finalizing the Althar series, specifically with the Opus Magnum, where we described in-depth for the first time what really happened to you when you incarnated, was a milestone, bringing forth this information into the public. It took a while for Joachim to assemble all the pieces that came in over time, over nearly a year, but then shortly before the workshop which occurred in March this year, where we spoke publicly about it for the very first time, all the pieces fell into their place.

When we brought up the topic of Uru, it was initially heavy, even dramatic, for there are so many memories woven into your DNA, woven into the blueprints that relate to the remembrance of Uru. But from there on, it went very, very fast, in that many humans took the chance to release Uru. They came across the books and read them. Meanwhile, seven, eight hundred people have read about Uru. They faced what happened in their very own way, they became aware of what happened, and by doing so a *tremendous*, tremendous overlay stemming from all of those events just vanished.

This does not mean that all the imprints that you have from these occurrences are totally gone, but it *does* mean that it is much easier for you to face them when your time comes to do so. So, that is really a milestone. The first milestone was being able to incarnate, the second milestone is to face what comes when you try to *release* the physical. We'll go in-depth into that discussion during this workshop.

We've just heard in the song, "We are waiting for the end." It's a bit like that for all those who are searching for enlightenment, isn't it? You're doing your thing, you're doing your studies, you're doing your practices, you're hoping, you're wishing, you are pretending... and in the end, you are "waiting for the end," for that one *big-bang-end* when suddenly you are enlightened, suddenly all your problems fall away, suddenly synchronicities are everywhere in your life, and all is just nice and shiny. But, sorry friends, this is *not the way it will go!* This is just not the way it will go.

Enlightenment only takes place in the moment, in the *now* moment and your only concern should be to be enlightened now. *Now!*

And there's every chance for you to realize full enlightenment in *this* very instant. So, never ever think again about the *next* instance and of course not about tomorrow, not about next year and not about time at all. This should be of no concern to you. Your concern should be *this very now moment!* I get passionate about this for there's so many ways humans distract themselves and they always claim they have understood everything, they have realized everything, blah blah blah blah, but then they fall back, as we've heard when you introduced yourself, into their patterns. Why is that? How come? Well, there are many reasons for that. But your concern should be to be enlightened in *this* moment and you can do that.

The moment you realize you are stuck in something, that is a moment of realization. It is the light within that says, "Hey, wake up! Now it's time to wake up. Now it's time to let go of the illusions." When you have that moment of enlightenment *you are beyond time.* Time doesn't exist anyway, but as a typical human, you hold on tightly to time. You have to catch the bus, you have to catch a flight, we begin here at a certain time. Yes, seen from within separation, time has a certain validity. Seen from the absolute, it is *nothing*, it doesn't exist. And you know that, time is a symptom of the dream.

So, if you have that split second of enlightenment in the now moment, you are immediately beyond time, *immediately* beyond time. Then you might even have the cosmic vision, the "I see how things truly are," what I call the Eye of Suchness. Just like that, no prerequisite. You just do it by a strong choice within not to delude yourself anymore, not to fall prey to illusions. You just let go and – *boom!* – a split second of enlightenment, you see things as they truly are.

Now, you might stay in that eternal moment as long as you like. There's no reason to go back. Most often though, you are in a way *pulled* back to your physical, to your biology and then you might look on your watch and see that just a minute has passed, or maybe a day, or maybe two weeks even, or just a split second. Actually, the duration does not matter at all, for *every* moment that you confirm that you are experiencing enlightenment within, you *confirm* the reality of it. And in each moment that you see true reality, the dream you are living in right now is weakening. The illusions are getting less strong.

The point will come where you just laugh constantly, mostly about yourself, for you will see all the illusions that you allow to direct your life.

You see them for what they truly are. And this is, in a sense, a short description of the road to enlightenment. It is about *illuminating your illusions,* nothing else.

Yes, I like to talk about wisdom and all the rest of that, but even the wisdom is only a means to illuminate your illusions. In that sense, even the highest wisdom is kind of an illusion which is only used to illuminate illusions that keep you stuck, and then that "helpful illusion" magically fades away, for you do not stick to it anymore. Use it for what it is – to illuminate your illusions.

Now, what happens when illusions are illuminated? Suddenly, you see pretty clear. The problem is that you have spent so many lifetimes in the physical and in the non-physical that there are piles and piles and piles of illusions and piles and piles and piles of patterns that even solidified into DNA and into what I call the non-physical blueprints. You hang on to them and they kind of drive your life. In a way it's good, because they sustain your physical life, but then it's not so good, because they keep you trapped in that very physical life. Illuminating the illusions just means that you let go of ever new layers, of ever new layers of illusions.

When you carry around a pile of heavy illusions and then you suddenly have an insight, an illumination of a given illusion which then just drops away, then you feel lighter, and say to yourself, "Ah! Twenty kilos suddenly went off my shoulders. Life is good, I'm done, I am enlightened," just to notice three months later that there is a pile of other illusions that are conditioning your life.

So, if you attempt to measure your progress, it will be very difficult. Hence, the wise advice is *not* to measure your progress. The wise advice is to only look at the now moment. Are you in illusions right now? Or are you choosing to observe what is going on, thereby detach from the illusions and hence make the patterns dissolve, because you do not enact them anymore.

We have many guests in this gathering. Very many, for it is indeed a celebration. A celebration of the fact that we have passed that most important milestone of releasing Uru. You might consider yourself sitting on a circular stage of an ancient amphitheatre. You know, all those old theaters have the stage in the middle and then you have ranks going up in circles around the stage and the spectators are sitting there and watching and kind of having fun with what's going on down there. Something similar is happening here. So often when you're on stage, you cannot see the audience because there's a blinding light, all the lights go on you so that everybody can see you, but you cannot see them. Sometimes, that's a blessing, so that you can pretend you're just doing your own thing, while in reality there are plenty of entities watching you. So the ranks are filled this day and they will be filled the next two days to come also.

With passing the second milestone, we came to the end of preparation. *The end of preparation.* You might say that all the rest that was done was *preparing*, preparing, preparing, providing wisdom here and there, providing some nurturing on the way, providing insights that kept you going, so that you can come to the point where you realize one of the major blocks that keep you stuck in physicality. And now that all this is done, now that all of this has been provided and we came to the end with the Althar series – meaning that all you need to know on a general basis to realize embodied ascension has been said –, *now it is all about you!* There is no preparation anymore. There is *no further final hint* that will catapult you to wherever. *There is none of that, so just do not wait for it!* You will not get it from the Althar series, *no way!* What you will get from Althar, from me, or from future workshops, is *true practice.*

You know that true practice is one of the three pillars that I've mentioned as being the most important of my messages. The other two pillars are represented by two groups that are here today in the audience. So, you might feel a bit into it. Don't be shy, you are the heroes on stage, they admire you. They come to honor you, to help you, to support you.

There's one group in particular that is Sananda. The group of Sananda holds one quality that is compassion. *True compassion* is one of the three major pillars that I – and those who work with me and us – envision as the most important ones. True compassion. They hold that quality, I would not say they embody it, but they have held that quality and whenever they appear that quality radiates out. As soon as they are radiating true compassion, as they do right now into this very spot – not because you need it, but as an honoring – you can easily get in resonance with it, so you can come very close to the true compassion that is already within yourself. It's not that you *need* any true compassion from the outside, not at all. But by them providing it and filling up the room with the quality of compassion, you can easily tap into your own. So that's why Sananda is here in big numbers.

And the same is true for the family of Uriel. Uriel represents the quality of *true wisdom* – the wisdom that leads beyond separation. Uriel is very, very intense, very intense. He comes close seldom because most people just cannot stand that clarity. They just cannot, they run away. And then they might attribute it to some mysterious god or whatever figure they prefer. So, Uriel oftentimes is a bit in the background. But today he is *very* prominent, today he is very prominent and he shines his light of true wisdom right into this gathering, so you can more easily get in touch with your own true wisdom, that is inherent in you, that is already there.

And then, of course, the third pillar is in the domain of the human – it is *true practice*. That is what it all amounts to. This is what's to come in the future. You want embodied realization? Well, then do it! But you *have* to do it, no one can do it for you. You want to get real? Or do you want to play along for the next twenty years? But nobody is getting younger, believe me, also mass consciousness is not getting easier to deal with. The moment the body gives you problems, everything will be more difficult. So, if you have a healthy day today, if you have a healthy second, well, why not get fully enlightened now? Why postpone? You want to wait for a magic wand? You are kidding.

True practice is in the domain of the human and the human has to do it. But the good thing is that this doing is a *non*-doing. It is not *achieving*, it is not *perfecting*, it is just *realizing* what you truly are. It's just reverting to pure consciousness. It is to *stop* doing, *stop* improving, *stop* waiting, *stop* wishing, *stop* everything. *Just stop with all the crap that you're doing right now* other than listening to me.

And that's not so easy, because you are always drawn back and pulled back into the rhythms of biology, into your daily needs. That's why you need true compassion. First and foremost with yourself, obviously. But it *is* difficult. If it was easy, everyone would do it, and we wouldn't be sitting here. But it's not. It hasn't been done often. So you need the utmost compassion for yourself.

And the highest compassion you can give to yourself is *not* to measure your progress, but only to say, "Wow, I just had a bright moment for I realized I was in illusions." That's wonderful.

15

than anybody should hope for. And
oright insight you can let go of whatever
and be in pure consciousness for an instance.
That is true practice.

True practice means *you become the master in your own house*, the house of the human. So often the body is misjudged. Yes, even I called it a prison, and it is. As long as you're not free to move in and out, then of course it's a prison. But at the same time, it's your temple in this reality. It is this temple that you want to inhabit consciously and use freely to be able to interact to your liking. So, you have to become the master in this house of yours. *You have to become the master of your thoughts, of your emotions, and of your feelings.* That means to become the master in your own house and you do it by true practice.

I have described true practice in detail in two non-exercises. The first is *cultivating your awareness*. Cultivating your awareness – this is something that we will do quite often here, mostly at the beginning of the various sessions. Cultivating awareness – this is the number one thing the human has to do. No one can give it to you. If you have no awareness, *nothing* will happen. You will just repeat the same things. Cultivating your awareness means, *you take time for yourself,* ideally in the morning, just after waking up. You sit down, shut up, and just observe. And whatever happens to you – you will be the observer. *You do not follow whatever comes.* No thought. No emotion. No feeling. No memory. You observe them for what they are and then you let them pass by. That means you become the master in your house.

What kind of a master is it, who runs after every thought, after every emotion, after every impulse? "I need this, I need that." Oh no, that's not a master, that's a zombie life, like everybody else lives. You are not here to live a zombie life, you're here to become *truly alive*.

So, become the master, cultivate your awareness. And it's not a doing, it has no prerequisite. You do not need to study any book, no philosophies, not even the Althar books. It is ancient. It's not even something special that is mentioned only here. Every tradition that ever explored the mysteries used that tool and the reason is that the moment you truly, truly, truly realize that you're not bound to whatever comes up within you, that you can step back, then you *decondition* yourself.

The moment you do not *react* to an impulse – you become free to *act*. You can choose to do anything, you're not *bound* to your conditioning anymore. This is the very way patterns are dissolved – *you do not enact them anymore*. That holds for the majority of the patterns that haunt you. There are others that might keep you alive in physicality, that's a bit different – you want to have a heartbeat, you want to breathe, okay. But so many other patterns that come as impulses, they bind you to a patterned life without freshness and bind you to the wheel of separation, to the Eye of Separation, as I call it.

17

And the second way of practicing is what I call *cultivating your light body*. It is an extension of the first exercise. It is helpful for anybody, but it's specifically helpful for those who are choosing to stay here after enlightenment. A typical human might ask, "Isn't that the normal choice?" No, not at all. It is not. Once you truly realize from beyond separation what goes on here, it's an absolutely ridiculous choice – wanting to come back if you could stay out? This is *not* "normal."

The primary reason for coming back, other than still having some illusions about enjoying physical life, is actually the compassion. The compassion. For you noted in your own life how seductive separation is, how difficult it is to get out of it even for a split second. And at some point you also notice how much help you personally have had from others. Be it a living person, dead masters or gurus, be it books, be it whoever. You had so much help. Without them, you would be truly stuck in the mud and you know that. This is the core reason why people choose to come back. And every second counts, every second counts that you reside here in separation as an enlightened being.

So, we will go deeply into the light body exercise. The light body exercise has a side effect. It will boil up everything that is in what I call the unconscious. Everything comes to the forefront. And with everything I mean everything that you have suppressed, that you did not want to see.

Apart from everything that is obviously in the unconscious, I will recap shortly, really shortly, the story of Uru and how you came to planet Earth, for this is so important to release. Thus, when I tell that story, I want you to *relive* it with me. It's not about rephrasing or telling it for a second, third, fourth time – that same old story – no, try to really *feel* what happened so that you can measure the impact that it had within you, deep within you, in your unconscious, in the DNA, in the blueprints, in the collective memory.

*

So, in the nonphysical was a time when entities already had eons of experiences, when they finally, finally came to the conclusion that they were just repeating the same old plots. Always the same stories played out with different non-physical forms, played out in various densities, in various disguises, in zillions of variants, but in the end it was always the same old plot. The plot of rise and fall and then we continue from the start.

This realization comes as a shock. If you truly understand this, if you truly feel into it, specifically if you're not bound to a single lifetime – as many humans still think and they have no true recollection of what happened before and what will happen in the future –, but if you are non-physical, if you don't know the notion of death and you have kind of a good overview of what happened, then this comes truly, truly as a shock. A standstill? Always the same? Ever the same? The same repetitions? No true creation? Nah, doesn't feel good. Imagine if you had to work at the same job for the next two hundred million eons and you go to the same office every morning or whatever you do. And even if it was going to the beach every morning for the next two hundred million eons. That's not so appealing.

So the moment that you truly realized what it meant that there was no true creation, you wanted to resolve that. And at that point the idea came up to try the incarnation approach. Physical matter was known at the time. Games have been played mostly *with* matter, but not so much *in* matter. So, Uru came up with the idea that it might be interesting to lower the vibration of consciousness to a degree that it could eventually act *as* matter, that you become so slow, so linear that you may truly understand what's going on.

Uru, being a part of the larger family of Uriel, has experimented with lowering the vibration of consciousness quite a lot, for they where, just as Uriel, very interested in what's going on in separation. How do these things work? What is polarity? What are the conditions of polarity, and most of all, how to get out? So they are called the *Master Scientists* for that very reason.

Those Master Scientists had experimented with compressing consciousness to an even denser level, seeing how that feels and then coming back from there. But they've noted from all the experiments that the compression they did was not sufficient in the sense that the entity who was compressed and then let go, did not have the required true "aha" realization of letting go. It wasn't deep enough, it was too easy to get out, it was just too easy.

Thus, they concluded the entity needed to be *truly lost,* just like the true selves in the very beginning when they entered separation. They have to be fully lost without knowing who they are, what they are, what they could do – fully lost. And *then* they need to find their way back by letting go.

That was the hope – nobody knew at the time if it would work out –, but the hope was that when this portion of consciousness was able to let go, to go beyond itself, this then would stimulate even their respective true self to let go of its very thin believe in being a separated entity.

So, it was decided to do the experiment. To make a long story short, Gaia prepared Earth and biological life forms. But then it came to the question, "How the hell do we get consciousness into these life forms?" They are like fire and water, they just don't match.

To achieve this, Uru's approach was taken. The approach consisted of two parts. First, a compression. A compression that takes a multidimensional, nearly unlimited being, a godlike being and compresses it to an amoeba, a small entity, figuratively spoken. So the compression had to be very, very strong. I like to relate it to human terms by using the analogy of an atomic explosion. You all know atomic explosions, the big mushroom cloud that emits from such an explosion. Now assume you are such a mushroom cloud, pretty huge. But then it has to go vice versa. That mushroom cloud is *compressed* back into density, into just a few atoms, a few kilograms, a very small volume. You are crushed, you are compressed into that very small volume with a force of an atomic explosion.

If a human is exposed to an atomic explosion, he is instantly evaporated, he just vanishes. Pfffft! Nothing left. Everything is pulverized, just gone. It's more or less the same when you do it vice versa. If you take that energy and compress such a multidimensional entity then, well, in a sense, that entity is gone. Meaning, it forgets completely who it is, where it came from, what where the causes, why did it volunteer to do such a crazy thing. And there was not just *one* compression like this, it was a *whole series,* it didn't stop.

Even though those who were the first wavers were informed about what was going on, even though Uru was a part of the initial group that went through that experiment, nobody could tell and nobody could predict what would really happen. Nobody could know if an entity that is undergoing this kind of treatment would survive or if it would become crippled for eternity. Nobody knew.

One side effect of the compression was a *tremendous* fear, a tremendous fear of undergoing it once again. And that fear then became projected on Uru, for Uru was the last you saw when you entered that metaphorical compression chamber. He was the last you saw. And then he closed the door and hid it, pushed the button, and then: *Boom!* Compression. *Boom!* Compression, and so on.

As a result, you have forgotten everything. You might say, your soul was squeezed out of you, your light was blown out, you forgot your name, you forgot all the good causes that made you volunteer to undergo this whole procedure. And, as if that wasn't enough, it was required that you truly *wanted* to be in the physical, so a portion of your already compressed consciousness was hypnotized, again by Uru. Hypnotized. Hypnotized to have the most intense desire to bond on the deepest level with the physical. Just like the neutrons and protons cling together with the energy that in the end creates the atomic explosion. With that very force you should cling to the particles, specifically to the atoms that make up your DNA.

And it worked out! It worked out and that was the first milestone. That was when incarnation finally *worked*. At some point you believed, "I am a body. I do not know where I come from. I have no idea of my capabilities. I have no idea of my name. I have no idea of any greater reality. I *do* know that I perceive things in a kind of sequence and that first and foremost I have to survive."

It was a big party on the other side – incarnation worked. But with the fear to meet Uru again came also a tremendous shame. Imagine, you are a multidimensional cosmic being and suddenly you are squeezed into something tiny, not knowing anything. You had a vague remembrance of some greatness of yours, but you really felt bad. That was shameful. No one should see you like that, not knowing who you are and where you came from. It was horrible, it was horrible. And it sits deep.

You might not encounter this on the conscious level right now, but when we will do the light body exercise, there will come a point when you might feel for the very first time a true shame that is associated with having a physical body. Many religions and traditions use that and make you feel bad. They say, "See! You have fallen from grace, you have a sinful body!" and all of that crap. They have completely twisted the whole notion and used it against you for power games. Still, there's a truth to it. But it's not because of a sin. It is that *shame* you felt. It's not because you did something wrong, but because you've volunteered to overcome the standstill. So, seen from the big picture, everything becomes relative.

Compression and hypnosis, that was the first milestone. And the second milestone that we have just passed – we will pass with this meeting, with this gathering and kind of have passed it with the previous gathering – is accepting that, it is letting go of that, it is seeing the whole picture of what has happened. By doing so, you release yourself from all the feelings of guilt and shame and specifically of fear.

So let us just take a few seconds here. Uru is very present in the outer ranks. He is here with us in person – some of you are from that very group – and in the non-physical, for they are still the Master Scientists. They're still highly interested to see and to assist and to support you in the next phase of embodied ascension.

Let's take a few minutes to allow Uru to become very present. Then, for yourself, let go of what you might attribute to Uru in terms of fear and in terms of shame of what it means to be in the physical.

*

In the end, it's always so easy. Once you are *aware* of something, then you can let it go. If you are *not* aware of it, then it comes from the unconscious and drives you without you noticing *what* drives you and thus you keep repeating the very same patterns.

This hypnosis from Uru – we will go deeply into its effects in the next session – but this hypnosis is one of the reasons why enlightenment is so difficult. Because at some point, you naturally come to a state where it is about letting go of the physical. It's just a natural step. You realize, *that's not you*. But then all kinds of weird things happen that pull you back. They come from the physical. Oftentimes it is truly the fear and the shame *disguised as something very urgent*. Then you have to move the body and do the next highly important thing, once again forgetting about letting go. But just being aware of this – being aware of when you are about to release your bond to the physical and change it into a conscious choice – being aware that at that point all kinds of distractions will come up, then you can see them for what they truly are and you can laugh with Uru, for he is with you right here.

Nothing of that was ever meant to happen, it was a byproduct. There's no need for fear, no need for shame, it just happened. That's the way it was. But now you can let go of that.

That is a true milestone and that is why I say that we come to the end of preparation. You are now – at least – *prepared* on a feeling level for what sooner or later will be *very real* for you.

We are here outside time and space. Whatever you'll experience at this workshop, you might say, is like a preview of what will come in true reality to you. It is real even now, yes, but there will come a point in your personal future where you will re–experience it *within* on a much more real, more personal level. Here, we do a preview, you get prepared for what is to come so that you're not shocked and can proudly just walk along as the master in your own house, greeting whatever comes, but not being distracted by anything.

So, let that sink in for a moment.

*

I greeted you as old friends, and old friends we all are. Whether you are here in person right now or whether you are reading the transcripts or you're listening to the audio, if you come across this material, you are an old friend. You wouldn't have made it so far. You wouldn't be attracted to this kind of crazy stuff if you wouldn't have been part of all the planning, processing, dreaming – dreaming is the right word – of all the dreaming.

Let's now take some time to greet each other without words, without the human facade of where do you come from and what do you do. Let's greet as in a true encounter. I do it at every meeting and it's always one of the very best occasions to come very close. To do so, partner up with a neighbor and place your chairs so that you see each other. Ideally, you start with someone you don't know.

Just close your eyes. We start with eyes closed. Take on a royal position, that means straighten your back, relax, truly feel your whole body.

Breathe through your nose. The breath just comes and goes at its own speed, you do not control anything. In fact, right now you are safe, you can let go of each and everything you want to control, everything. This might be the safest place in all of the Universe right now.

There are so many things humans do not want to see about themselves. They hide it. They push it away. They tell themselves that it's not there, even though they know better. Sometimes it's even easier to see these hidden gems in another person. Yes, there are ways to hide something, but this kind of stuff, well, you can't really hide. Those with eyes to see will see, there's no way to hide it. So why even try? Instead, why not open up and show all that you are, allow the other to see *all* that you are. Because you all had so many lifetimes and so many experiences, there is certainly nobody here who is only good or bad. You have played on all sides, all the time. But did it really happen? Or was it just a dream? Dream figures, dream places, shadow dances. Maybe all of that was not that serious?

So, when you're ready, you slowly open your eyes. Glance softly into the eyes of the other, without staring, just accepting. The eyes are the gateways to what humans call the soul. Do not hide anything, there's no reason to hide it. Do not be repulsed by anything you see (chuckles). There is nothing in the other that you don't have also, believe me.

One caveat here. If you truly let go of the control, you might see that your partner changes their shape. The face might change, shapeshifting into another human, a man or a woman, a black, a yellow guy, an alien even. Don't get distracted by that. You all have a long history in all kinds of forms, so greet everything that you meet.

*

So please, if you are ready, open your eyes.

*

Open your awareness. Realize that you are much larger than your physical body.

*

Just for the fun of it, smile. See what that changes. Don't be serious.

If it's an alien shape, let it smile also. Or not. (laughs)

*

Try to hold that awareness and openness while you move your body and stand up.

Give a hug to your partner and change to the next one.

* * *

That was a good encounter, wasn't it? Things can be so easy. So we close the session.

I am Althar, looking forward to see you in the next session. Thank you.

2. Journey Into the Unconscious

We start with cultivating the awareness. Whenever you cultivate your awareness, take on a royal position as I call it. Royal position means straightening the backbone. Ideally, your backbone is upright for then you do not need to exert any muscle power to stay stable. The more you bend to one side or you let your head bend, you need muscles and then after five minutes, everything gets tense. But if you sit upright, the shoulders can relax, you let them fall down, the breathing can go down, the belly can move. You do not need any muscles to hold that position. Plus, there is a correlation between the physical body, the emotional body, and even the mind. It always goes in both directions. When you take on a position of clarity which means an upright position, then it spreads out. The mental becomes clear, the emotional also becomes clear. Usually, it's the other way around. You become agitated, because something disturbs you, you have some emotions that you don't like and then the body and muscles react, you may make fists, whatever you do when you are getting emotional.

We are doing it the other way around. We start with the physical body in an upright position and take advantage of this correspondence with the emotional and the mental bodies.

You breathe through the nose without any wish to control your breath, and this is really not easy. If you just follow your breath, just observe how deep the breath is, you will most often feel how it gets stuck somewhere in your upper chest area. Then you wonder why there is a blockage? You want to push that blockage away or breath through it. Don't do that, just observe. Place your awareness in that area and you will discover a miracle: Wherever you place your awareness, that portion of your body will relax. It will just relax, it will open up. It might take a while. But sooner or later, it will just open up. This works *everywhere* in your body.

So, when I say, "Become aware of your *whole* body" – it is actually not that easy, but also not that difficult – it also means your whole body gets relaxed, just like this, without you doing anything, without you chanting mantras or telling yourself affirmations. Just by the nature of your very awareness and by being aware of your body, your body relaxes.

*

After you've taken on a straight position, feel your body weight – that's the easiest way to really gather everything of you within your body. Just feel your body weight, feel how your feet press on the floor, feel the weight of your legs pressing on the floor. Just be aware of that.

Now, at the same time be aware how your whole body presses on the chair with your buttocks. Stay aware simultaneously of your feet, your buttocks, and your legs.

You will notice immediately the difference when you do it just mentally – in the sense of telling yourself, "Aha, I feel my legs, I feel my buttocks, I feel both of them" – versus you just *feel* them. Because the mental can only do one thing at a time. It cannot do both. It would flicker back and forth. But you can *feel*, you can *sense* a lot of things at the same time.

Now feel your hands. Your arms. Your whole chest.

Feel the lips of your mouth. They are extremely sensitive. They are completely wired with your emotional body. The facial expression corresponds most often to your emotional body. Some people can fake it, but most cannot.

Be aware of how the air enters your nose when you breathe.

Feel your eyes and your skull.

There's a good reason that in mostly all traditions the body plays an important role when it comes to meditation, to the practice of awareness. Simply, because the body is always there. You can always feel it. So, whenever you are out there in your dreams and you want to ground yourself, just do this simple exercise. *Feel* your body, *feel* your breath, stop thinking, stop chasing your dreams, memories and thoughts. And immediately things will calm down.

Let's be quiet for a minute or two. You just observe what's penetrating to the surface of your awareness.

*

One might think, "If I were good at this then nothing would pop up into my awareness." That is just totally wrong. The only thing in which you could be "good" at is *not to follow* what pops up into your awareness.

You had an intense day today, not only the journey here, but also the encounter in the first session. Many things have been stirred up. There are billions of ideas, false memories, and impulses swirling all around you. There's nothing bad with that – it's just natural. But to become a master of your own house means that you are able to just observe, to not be carried away by *whatever* shows up.

As soon as you notice you have been carried away, true compassion will allow you to simply return to the seat of the observer and be aware once again, without any regret. That is cultivating your awareness. That is freeing yourself from all the impulses and patterns. The freer you get, the more you approach the free human, the free being. You don't even need to be an "enlightened" being, it doesn't even matter. You will notice instantly the difference, "Do I *act?* Or are my buttons just pushed and I *react* like a robot?" This in itself is a grand blessing, if you are able *not* to react, but to observe, to let go, and then to act as you would like.

Still, the question comes up, "Where do all these impulses and thoughts and memories come from? And how many of them do I even recognize? Many of them are so subtle. But I only realize that they exist when I start reacting." And that's true. That's very true. But the more you get used to this most simple non-practice, the more you will tune into the finer levels of your awareness.

Then, rough thoughts, rough concepts, ideas and impulses from the more waking consciousness will not distract you so much any more. You will see the finer impulses on the finer levels. Quite obviously, the earlier that you notice you have gone astray, the easier it becomes to let it go. Think of a hot summer. An unaware human has a walk in the woods and he's smoking, throws away a cigarette and then he notices, "Oops! It starts burning." So he can easily just extinguish the fire by trampling on it and it will be gone. But if he doesn't do that, if he lets it burn and spread, then suddenly you have a burning Amazon. This is very hard to control. It is the same with all of your emotions. The earlier you become aware of them, the easier it is to let them go before they even unfold.

But this is a fruit that comes over time. The core point is, never judge yourself as being good or bad at this. Good or bad is not the point. The point is to be as good as you can be, that's all that counts.

Tomorrow, we will dive deeply into the light body exercise. And the light body exercise – when done correctly – is very intense, actually, extremely intense. You might say, it boils up the unconscious. Everything that resides there is scared up, comes to light. And not everything down there wants to be exposed to the light.

Thus, today we will take you on a journey into the unconscious, as *visitors*, as *observers*. We do not go there to heal anything, to repair or to release, nothing like that. We just go there as observers. You might say, we go as pure consciousness. Think of a museum. "It was like this when humans existed. They had the unconscious and look, here are certain areas, certain departments where memories are stored. And this is what was driving them all along and they didn't even know it. Because it was disguised as subtle impulses." So we go there and we go very, very deep as observers, as pure consciousness.

We will hear a bit of music, then we'll bring in Althar and he'll guide us through the unconscious. When I say "the unconscious", I mean we will go as a group, but everybody will go into its own unconscious. Such are the wonders of consciousness, we can do these things. So it's very safe and still it's very personal.

*

(Music plays)

I am Althar the Crystal Dragon!

We've done many trips in the previous workshops. We've dived into the sun, we went deep into matter and beyond, we went into all the magnitudes of time, but the unconscious is my favorite.

We're going to do a deep, deep trip into what humans call the unconscious. And with unconscious I mean all that eludes your waking awareness, but still influences you. And there is a lot, for you had many, many, many experiences throughout all the eons of your existence in separation. Whatever was too harsh, whatever you could not devour, whatever you weren't able to stand, because maybe it was too brutal or even too beautiful, was pushed away. Pushed into what is now called the unconscious. But pushing something away does not mean that it is out of existence. It is still there.

You can view many of these things that you pushed away as events which are trapped inside small time capsules. They are like small strips of a movie which are played over and over again, enacting the ever same scenes. It can be a very small event or it can be a whole lifetime that ended dramatically for whatever reason.

Everything that you were not able to stand was pushed down there. You might see this as all kinds of things, as memories, but also, in a way, they are like "entities," not like you, but beings that have a limited consciousness that is only mirroring itself, going in circles and while doing so, they give off a scent, a stink, you could say. That odor rises up, it penetrates to the surface and colors the perception of your so-called waking consciousness. So you might rightfully ask when perceiving something, are you perceiving objectively the surrounding and what is in front of your eyes or is it, to a large degree, your past? For everything that you perceive is interpreted and colored by what comes from down there, from the unconscious.

So often these suppressed memories, events, and occurrences do *not* want you to do a specific thing, because they do not want to experience it again. So they whisper, "Do not do that again!", and then you find a rational reason that says, "No I won't go there". But the true decision was not made consciously by you.

This is similar to what you have just experienced when sitting down and observing what's coming to the surface from within you. Where did it come from? Who or what – what instance within you – defines what's to follow? Mostly, it's fully automatic. And obviously, even if you're doing something, even if you are in an interaction, even if you are in your work, all of these things *permanently* come up from the unconscious.

It's not that just because we sat down and observed, suddenly they started bubbling to the surface. No! They're constantly, constantly, constantly transpiring their scent, their wants and needs and "don't wants" and "don't needs", their desires, and fears. All of these are then transformed by you into an image of the present and taken into account while you believe you are making a free choice. So much for free choices.

On this trip, we will visit various important areas of the unconscious that hold memories of what you experienced in the past – beautiful and ugly – so as to become aware of their existence. Oftentimes, just being aware that they exist makes life so much easier. And as has been said before, we go there as observers, we go there as pure consciousness from *beyond* time. We do not go as healers or the wise uncle or anything like that. We just go there and inspect. Everybody inspects his own unconscious, visits it, says, "Hello, here I am", but without interfering. Just to become aware of it.

We will go deeper and deeper and deeper. We will come to the very core of your existence. And as it happens to be, the very core of your existence is actually the very core of the whole Second Round of Creation. It's quite a trip.

In the setup that we have chosen, we use a lot of images, of course, to make the words a bit more palpable so you can better feel them. Some of you may have the gift of seeing visuals to make it a bit more alive.

In our set up, just imagine that you are on the surface of an ocean. The sun is shining. There are a few waves, nothing disturbing is going on. You feel absolutely confident in yourself. Everything is fine. You are there as consciousness. We are hovering at the surface of the ocean above a volcano which is at the ground level of the sea. We are just above the opening of that volcano. Entering the volcano is the symbol for moving into the unconscious. The shaft that goes directly down into the earth is called the "vent" of the volcano, the vent. I will use this term frequently. That is where we go down. And happily, it is full of water, so there is no risk that any magma spills out and gives you another sauna effect like we had before. (It was very hot during the whole day.)

So, get ready. Enter the water as consciousness. Luckily, consciousness does not need to breathe, no problem with that. Just dive down. It's also cool and fresh, if that makes sense. And just go deeper, let yourself sink, sink, sink down, deeper into the water, into the various depths of consciousness. You know, I often use the ocean as a metaphor for consciousness, so we are diving into consciousness.

As you get deeper everything gets dim, a bit foggy, the light goes away. Even weird creatures show up, the weirdest fish you've ever seen, quite like aliens. We just go deeper and deeper and we sink down, down to the volcano opening.

*

(Music starts playing and accompanies all that follows)

Come with me, enter into that volcano, into your personal unconscious. Into the vent of the volcano. From the vent halls branch of, caves, and chambers that hold so many memories, important memories that influence you at all times.

The first hall that we are going to visit is the Hall of the Non-Physical Life Forms. You had plenty of those. Non-physical forms. *No pain.* Can you imagine that? No physical body means no pain. Grandiose lifeforms, for eons and eons. We are going deeper, approaching the gate to the Hall of the Non-Physical Life Forms. When you're in there, open up to the memories, even to the imagination. Feel how it was, for there is a vague remembrance. Are you intrigued by dragons? Well, guess where the memories of the dragons reside.

*

(A sound indicates when a hall is entered and left.)

So many eons you have spent as non-physical beings. Glorious it was at times. How was life as a light fog? Floating, expanding. As a dragon even? No need to feed yourself. No true need to protect yourself. Still, games have been played in the other realms. You call it wars these days. But a war without a physical body is something special. You cannot be hurt? Then war is relative.

It was here that you discovered the standstill, the absence of true creation. You realized here, in the non-physical that in separation *there is no true creation.* Everything repeats.

Oh, you have visited so many realms, so many densities. But at some point you realized – *repetitions*, it is all repetitions of the ever same games.

And it drives an entity mad. It was a shock to realize the standstill, a true shock which sits deep.

Sometimes, humans are longing for the non-physical realms, they want to go back. They even feel approached by non-physical beings that want to lure them to come to their side. But I'll tell you, if you want enlightenment, don't go there. *You came from there!* You want to get out *at the other end of the tunnel.* If such an entity approaches you, you might want to tell it about enlightenment, about presence, about true wisdom, about separation, about letting go.

Allow yourself to feel the eras of your non-physical existence. They are a bit remote. Sometimes it's difficult for a human to relate to them, because all the sensory perception was very different, but it's still there, even though it's vague, it's still there.

Imagine a fight in the non-physical, at lightning speed.

And the joy. Huh. Good.

Let's leave that hall and move deeper. Deeper into your unconscious. Recall that we are here as observers. We go back to the vent of the volcano and go deeper.

*

You decided to incarnate into biological life forms and the very basis of the biological life forms are the individual cells. Thus, we go into the Hall of Single-Cell Organisms.

The human body consists of 10^{14} cells. If you would line them up in a thread, you could wind that thread sixteen times around planet Earth. You are a walking pile of cells. You have the same amount of... even more cells within you that do not carry your DNA. That is your personal mass consciousness that you carry with you all the time. And these cells have a life of their own. Let's see how that life is. Let's go into that Hall of Single-Cell Organisms, the very basis of your physical existence.

*

Feel into an amoeba, somewhere in the dark, maybe in some liquid, floating around. What are the sensory impulses it gets? A bit of touch. It might react to light, but there is not much more. But still that cell wants to live. It wants to maintain its form, so it has to feed on something. Sometimes it just eats some molecules that are swirling around, but oftentimes cells feed on other cells.

Cell doesn't complain about anything. It's not discussing anything. It doesn't do philosophy. It is just there. It wants to create offspring to maintain itself.

The consciousness that incarnated was injected into the atoms of the DNA and from there it took over the thought patterns of the larger compounds, like the cells. Thus, the incarnated consciousness thought, "Oh, I'm not only matter, I'm also a cell and I want to live, I want to feed, I want to reproduce, I want to maintain what I am."

If at one point you want to go beyond the physical, you will find that this part of your consciousness will absolutely veto you. It has a different agenda. "Letting go of me being a cell, of my 'cellness'? That means being wiped out, *so you don't dare go out there!* For I am programmed to live, and I know I am a cell. I've been hypnotized into believing 'I am a cell', so nobody goes anywhere. And I'm stronger than you, *as you know*. You cannot even stop breathing for five minutes, I would *force* you to continue breathing!", says the cell and all its companions.

Then the cells built up, created more complex organisms, tissues, organs, complex biological lifeforms. The embedded consciousness of you, in a way, grew with it, expanding its identity. But the cell is still your basis.

They are fascinating. You can study an individual cell for an eon, but let's not do that, let's not go into the details. Let's go to the core.

So slowly, slowly come out of that hall, come back to the vent and go deeper.

*

The next hall we are going to visit is called the Hall of Predators. The predators. Man is a predator. He kills all the time to feed himself. And the imprints that all the animals have, the memories, they are also within the human, they came along the DNA strands. They were *intense*.

When we do the light body exercise, when you do it in the weeks and months to come, you might have remembrances of that strong physical power and you want to run out and dominate. To dominate might also mean starting the next great project. But don't do that, observe where that comes from.

Power is seductive, physical strength is seductive. Being able to dominate is *so* seductive. And you all did it. As animals, of course, but as humans even more. So let's spend some time in the hall and relive some of those memories that are buried and held there.

*

Imagine yourself to be, say, a tiger at the height of its physical strength. It's roaming around. It's hungry, it wants to *hunt*. It has smelled its prey and is following it. Be that tiger for a moment, feel that body moving as you want. With great speed, you are agile. It's so much fun to be in such a body. You *know* you are strong, you *know* your prey is weak. But still, each hunt is dangerous, for you might be injured and each injury could be deadly. So you have to be very present. All your skills are required. Still, it's so seductive.

So you run after the prey. It tries to escape, but you know you are fast. Feel that. A final sprint, you jump and hit the prey. You bite into its throat as you did so often. You taste the blood. You absorb the life force energy of that entity. That is *glorious!* You've won once again and fed your-self. You are still in the game. You can even feed your offspring. Biology is satisfied. Ah, raw power is good, it's intense. And whatever is in-tense finds its imprints into the blueprints and the DNA, consciousness in separation wants repeti-tion of the intensity. That's how it works.

But as each predator knows only too well, "Sooner or later, I will age and I will be eaten my-self." So, even though here is a lot of power mem-ories, there is a lot of fright and pain also. Being killed, having lost the fight, lost against a younger one, faster one, more skilled one, stronger one. Thus, relaxing in that realm is not that easy.

All of these memories are buried within you. "Run or fight, what do you choose?" And they penetrate to the surface, coloring your decisions, your perceptions, your choices. It's a wild life, it's an *intense* life.

*

Let's move on and go deeper. The halls we have visited so far might feel a bit distant. The non-physical life forms, cells... the animals are maybe closest to you. But now we approach the Hall of your Personal Aspects.

Everything that you have suppressed found its way here. Everything. It's in its personal time capsule. Be it the spider on your pillow, a scold-ing adult, being raped or abused, or you doing this to others knowing that one day it will catch you, it will return to you. All this sank down here, deep, deep into the unconscious. It is a zombie land. The land of the dead. So be prepared, this is your personal Hall of Aspects. Go as an observer. Do not heal, do not do anything other than being present and observe.

*

All these aspects, they are like ghosts. Floating around, caught in their own thoughts and memories. The same event being played over and over again.

You did something wrong or so somebody else thought so and thus shouted at you, belittled you. Oh, it was too much, you've felt ashamed. You put it as an aspect here, never to do it again, for you do not want to experience this ever again.

Feel into shame. It makes you small, it paralyzes you. You want to cut off all relationships to the outside, for you do not want anybody to mirror this feeling of shame to you, so you close up and send this aspect down here. It is reliving this experience over and over again and while doing so, it radiates its fear, its anger and thus colors your perceptions. It relives it over and over, wanting to come to resolution, but it cannot find it, for it is limited, it is cut off.

You also carry a lot of packages from other lifetimes that ended up here. There are so many ways not to end a lifetime graciously. On the battlefield, on the sickbed, pestilence, leprosy. Or you were on your path to awakening and made the mistake to talk about it and somebody felt that you had to be burned, or quartered, or beheaded, or stoned to death. This is not pleasant. This ends-up down here, *including* the causes that led up to it. So you might believe, "Awakening is danger-ous, *better don't do it!"* and this transpires to your waking consciousness.

Here you can truly see that time is not linear. These creepy beings here, if you want to call them beings, they reexperience the same time capsule over and over again. They do not even see each other, they only see their own misery.

Some might recognize you. They might come close, they feel your light, they feel a potential of themselves that they could become. Be in true compassion, do not interfere, that is not your job.

Good. Let's move on. Back into the vent of the volcano and we go deeper.

*

The next hall we are going to visit is the Hall of the Collective Aspects. This is the backdrop of whatever you experience in separation, the collec-tive aspects. Many experiences were intense, thus they were imprinted in the blueprints and the DNA. They represent the stage on which you play. It's a kind of mass consciousness that goes way, way back to the very beginning of existence in separation, covering all intense experiences that were ever made.

So be prepared. This hall is like a time travel in itself. The memories held here are always present. All these time epochs call out to you and transpire into your waking consciousness at all times.

*

How many cultures have been here on Earth that don't exist anymore?

How many peoples have existed here on Earth that do not exist anymore?

How many empires have there been, how many epochs?

You all know that everything comes and goes, rises and falls. That is the collective experience. You've been around as your true self and now as an incarnation of your true self since the very beginning. *You know it all!* Such are the collective memories.

How much hope has there been?

How many religions, philosophies?

But nothing, nothing, nothing ever brought you lasting peace or freedom. No matter how sophisticated or vicious it was, no matter how successful it appears to have been. No matter how long it lasted.

Egypt lasted about 3000 years. And where is it now? Look at it. It's a pity.

The second World War. Just a blink of time away. It has left so many imprints and you all sitting here know that – imprints in your parents and grandparents, in what the countries think about each other, how they act. Even though it ended seventy years ago, it still plays out in the dreams of those who fell in the war. They came back, those who were slaughtered. They have reincarnated and brought their memories with them. But it has also been imprinted in the collective memory.

Of course, Atlantis. The archetype of downfall, for it was the very first high culture humans are aware of. There was so much hope and even breakthroughs in consciousness. But then – oops – it collapsed. The whole Earth took a full cycle to recover from that. That sits deep, that's the collective remembrance.

And that's why you are here, that's why you have incarnated, that's why you hold the dream of embodied ascension. Yes, it took a while. But what is "a while" if you face the standstill? It took so much experience, for nobody knew how separation would play out. It needed to be experienced, and it was experienced. And here is the library of that.

Whatever rises will fall. Nothing ever brought lasting peace.

Nothing brought true creation.

You are here as pure consciousness, you observe. So you are not getting drawn into it. That is very important.

Let's leave this hall.

*

You are here to overcome the standstill on a personal basis and, as a byproduct, for all of existence. But to do that, you have to pass that compression chamber.

Even though you might have released Uru on some conscious level, it is wise that we pay a visit to what we call metaphorically the compression chamber. It is ahead of us. We're approaching the compression chamber where you were compressed and hypnotized so that you can bond with physical matter under the belief – not to say spell – under the belief "I am a body." And you did it on behalf of your spiritual families. It was a glorious deed, a bit crazy, but the best choice we had at the time.

So, let's go there as observers. Everything that is related to Uru, the compression, fear and shame is stored here. Become aware of it, don't be overwhelmed by it.

*

This buzzing which can be heard in the music symbolizes the hypnosis at the micro level of your consciousness that bonded with subatomic particles.

"I am physical. I am matter, yes! I have a form. I want to live!"

Here, in the compression chamber, you saw how Uru locked the door. Then suddenly the compression set in with the force of an atomic explosion. Cruel. Horrible. Shocking. Suffocating. Dreadful. Nobody could imagine that. Nobody could. But then it happened (sound of an atomic explosion in the background).

And what was once a proud entity wanting to go down to Earth as a pioneer of consciousness, suddenly was blown out, condensed to a speck of dust. The veiling set in. You *forgot*. You forgot the reason why you came here. You didn't understand what was going on. Nobody could imagine such a force. And it continued. There was a series of these compressions that took place on you. They squeezed out the very soul of you, your name, your light. The veiling became denser and denser. It wouldn't end. It wouldn't end.

Uru was the last you have seen. He pulled that trigger. So he became the symbol of incarnation and therefore the symbol of letting go of incarnation.

How often in all of your lifetimes have you been close to releasing the physical, but then something kicked in? Remembrances of fear and shame. Doesn't matter how it expressed itself, but it came from this chamber.

What if Uru comes around and compresses you even stronger and sends you once more into eternal damnation in physical matter? So, better not try to release the physical. Thus, you stayed and stayed.

Now, we're here as pure consciousness. The interpretation you gave while being in that chamber was wrong. As mostly everything in separation is just wrong. It was a wrong interpretation from a false standpoint.

Seemingly very real when you are trapped in separation – just a dream when you're outside.

Here, we are as pure consciousness, revisiting those memories without being drawn into them, preparing you to face them when they come up in whatever disguise.

Let's leave that chamber and go even deeper.

*

Let's go to the very core of you. Sink deeper.

What is at the core of you? Feel into that. What could that be? We are approaching it, we are sinking deeper. But we are sinking as pure consciousness. We use the Eye of Suchness, that way we can observe without being drawn in. That's the blessing of pure consciousness, that's the blessing of knowing who you are.

There is just one reason, one root cause for the whole Second Round of Creation and thus for you and for everything else. It's the very root cause and *here* the healing has to be applied, nowhere else. All the rest is just symptoms. All the rest, all that we have just seen in the various halls are symptoms of this one root cause.

In a single lifetime you may be able to heal an aspect or two, maybe twenty. What about the other ten thousand? *You have to realize the root cause!* Not on a mental basis. Not on a basis that says, "I agree." But you have to *feel* it. And that's why we are here.

The one root cause is, of course, the belief in separation. It's like a pulse. (distorted booming pulse in the background)

Who am I?

Who am I?

When consciousness pondered the idea of separation, it built a shell around itself. And suddenly it was cut off by this imaginary shell. And it felt, "Oh, somehow I am, but *who am I*?" And in order to answer the question "Who am I?" that imprisoned consciousness needed to mirror itself.

And so it did, and so it did, and so it did. It has mirrored itself by applying separation over and over again. Creating more details. Taking the ever same building blocks and arranging them in new manners, experiencing them. But then... This is separation, this is polarity. *Here, nothing is permanent.* Whatever mirror it created, sooner or later it was destroyed, it faded. So it needs constant, constant, constant re-validation.

That is the one root cause of the Second Round of Creation!

If you look at humans, all the problems humans have you can track down to one single root cause. Humans would call it a lack of self-esteem, a lack self-worth. They have to compensate for that and thus they do all the crazy things they do all the time. But here you can realize, "Wait a minute, we're talking about self-worth. But that apparent imagined "self" has no *reality*. It is *false in itself.* It is false *from the outset*. It doesn't even exist! So how could there ever be self-esteem? There is none!"

And thus it goes on and on. For even if you realize the falseness of self, there is the fear that if you stop mirroring yourself, stop pretending to create self-esteem, then you will be wiped out. You have the fear of going out of existence.

That's the trick with separation. It encapsulates itself in a time bubble, it does so everywhere on every level of the so- called consciousness in the Second Round of Creation. It's always the same. Each boom (as heard in the background) might be a whole eon, an epoch. Rise and fall of a culture. The creation and decay of a particle. Time does not play any role in separation. It's always the same on all levels.

But here we sit, we can observe and *we can see things as they truly are.* With the Eye of Suchness.

Nothing that came from separation defines you in any way!

These are all just remnants of dreams. Dreams pretending to be real, dreams fighting for life, but then, tumbling once more. That is the nature of separation. Enough is not enough. The taste of repetition. Until one day, one moment you decide, "Enough!" (pulse in the background stops)

When the Eye of Suchness does not sleep, the various dreams fade away.

And where do dreams go when you wake up? Does it even matter?

Now, after all this drama, all the cultures, all the life forms, all the experiences – what is real? Is it worth repeating that and repeating that? Oh, you did! And nobody forces you to do anything, but here you have a *choice*. Do you allow this understanding of separation to become reality for you? Or is it just a nice concept, just another idea to interpret reality? That's up to you. But you wouldn't be here, if you came for playing or just another theory. Instead, it's about letting go of each and every theory. No theory ever brought anybody anywhere. But here, as pure consciousness, applying the Eye of Suchness, here, now, in this very sacred moment, you can *see things as they truly are.*

You can see the dream for what it truly is!

I said in the beginning that this is kind of a preview of what you will experience at a later point. But maybe it's even absolutely real right now for you. It is you, who decides that. But at the deepest core, at the deepest, deepest core of yourself, at some point you have to witness that separation is not real. And with that the dream will fade. Then, you'll have cured it at the root. You'll have set yourself free.

Embodied ascension, the most crazy attempt of all, literally, is to realize this, but then to go back into separation consciously, to maintain a body in the dreamlands of separation. Well, you might pretend you are doing this to have some more fun in your life as a human, but after five minutes or, say, five weeks at most, you'll notice, well, this is not that compelling. Because, hey, here is the Third Round of Creation, here is *true creation.* Do you really think that walking the beach with a Mai Tai in your hands is the greatest thing you could ever experience? It's not.

So, when you go back, it's because of true compassion for those who are still trapped. Knowing that you've had so much help along your way. And also knowing that you will not actively do anything. Just your presence is enough. Just your presence is enough.

By doing this, by choosing the Eye of Suchness to see things as they truly are, you immediately are at this point where we are right now. Choosing the Eye of Suchness ends that pulse of separation everywhere and says, "Ha-ha, without me, please. I am not *in* the dream. I'm *observing* the dream. Leave me alone, stupid dream." And as you do that, you change the blueprints, you leave a big trail in the blueprints for all the species to find the exit door easier. For does it really need to be *so* difficult to leave separation? So dreadful, so painful?

As an engineer, I say, no it doesn't need to be, it was kind of a weird design. But that's the way we implemented it. Now we have to live with the consequences and try to improve things. That's what humans do all the time and we do the same here. And the best improvement that we came up with is, well, "Lit the exit door! Show that it *can* be done. Then letting go will become easier and easier. With every day and with every generation."

Also, once you truly have understood the mechanics of separation, well, then you are free to truly *act* within the dream. There is no need to have a bad dream. What about a *happy* dream? You realize you are free. You do not need to feel what a limited human feels. You are free in what you want to feel. Even if you see horrible things, well, it's still a dream. You do not have to feel pity for anything. But still you can act and help those who are within the dream, knowing that one day they will also wake up and realize everything as what it is – a dreamland springing from an absurd idea – "being separated."

I will leave you with a final statement.

There is absolutely no need for you to go back into your human mode, into your human limitations. Actually, what we are doing in this workshop – now that the preparation has ended – we're establishing what I call a "bridgehead in the Third Round of Creation."

A bridge connects two sides, and the pillars on the ends are called the bridgeheads. The term is sometimes used when two parties are battling and they're trying to cross a river. Then creating a bridgehead is very difficult. You have to hold it, you have to build a bridge so that others can cross the river.

Now, the bridgehead we are going to build here in the Third Round of Creation is certainly not anything of brick and mortar, not at all, and it is not in any way that the Third Round of Creation would repulse you. But there's a pull from the other side, a pull from separation that wants to pull you back in. Thus, creating a bridgehead here means the true wisdom within you has to find deep, deep, deep roots that go deep into the Third Round of Creation. You are the first to do that as a group.

I never mentioned this before, although we've been here before, but now it's time to get real. It's *so* time to get real. That bridge *is more real than anything.* And it goes right into dreamland. It is personal for you and it is, in a way, collective, for it changes the blueprints.

Nobody will walk your bridge. It's yours alone, that's for sure. But if the bridgehead is created at the same time by many people then it will be much easier for you to maintain that bridgehead. So, in a sense, *please* feel free to stay here forever with a portion of you while you let the rest of you experience dreamland through the human physical body.

This was a long day, a hot day. Even without magma, it was quite hot. I do wish that you could sleep tonight. At a certain point though you better don't sleep at all. Even in your dream you shouldn't sleep, if that makes any sense.

But I wish to greet you tomorrow refreshed, no matter how you realize that. Maybe you should dream of becoming refreshed.

I am Althar. I am *very* proud and honored to have you here and share with me this ride. And, by the way, all the spectators are cheering and applauding you. We'll meet again tomorrow, thank you.

3. The Light Body Exercise

(sitting in silence for a few minutes)

We have much on the plate for today, and right now we are bringing it in. So, you might sense instantly – even without being able to put it into precise words – what is going to happen today and what you might experience. And then, throughout the day, we will bring it into this physical realm so you can play it through with your human body, your human sensory devices and all the other parts and pieces of your consciousness.

*

You might feel that the air is getting thicker.

Also, the spectators are with us again. They are eager to see what's happening today for we will go deep and we will do some experiments.

(Music: "Will The Sun Ever Rise?" from *Five Finger Death Punch*)

I am Althar, the Crystal Dragon!

Will the sun ever rise? What do you think? No, it cannot. It was always there, it never moved. It is just the sun. It's like your pure consciousness. Will your pure consciousness ever rise? No! It hasn't moved. It hasn't even changed.

This piece of music is really beautiful in many respects. First, the lyrics are very appropriate for what we're doing here. "One step forward, two steps back" – isn't that the feeling that you have when you are on your road to enlightenment?

Once in a while you feel a huge relieve, a breakthrough, you think, "Now, here it is! Now I'm *done!* I'm *relieved*, I'm *free*, I feel *good*", only to notice a few days or weeks later – "Nah, not yet" and then a kind of depression may come in. Then it feels like you're going two steps back and you don't really know what's going on with all of this enlightenment business.

Separation is very sticky, it's like flypaper. You see it sticking to your right hand, and you try to rub it away, suddenly it's gone, and you're happy, but then you look at your left hand and there it sticks. And so it goes on and on – or so it seems.

"If you had seen what I've seen, then you will notice – nothing is clean", as the lyrics said. Absolutely! For nothing that you see and perceive in separation is undistorted. The very act of perceiving is a distortion of reality. Full stop.

Whatever you can see is distorted. You never see things as they truly are through your physical senses! No way! They are just not made for this. They are made to solidify separation, and by applying them over and over again you do just that – you get yourself deeper into separation. Which is fine for a while. But as soon as you discover the repetitions and the standstill, then it's not that fine at all. You want to get out.

This piece of music is also very nice, because it covers the whole range of musical expression, from very tender music, gentle even, too harsh and rough, roaring and dramatic – all is in there.

Just like with the human who covers the whole spectrum of consciousness. A human can reach to the very highest consciousness, the pure consciousness, to the bliss of pure consciousness, and down to the other end of the spectrum. Embodied in physicality, it can go as deep as the dumbest consciousness, barely noticing anything, just surviving, living somehow, without being aware of anything.

You find all of these expressions amongst the humans. You find the highest entities, the wisest walking in a body as well as the lowest, and somehow they appear to look the same, having two arms and two legs and kind of a nose. But, are they really the same? Or is it just an outer expression of them, while within they are, well, not that different, but they focus on very different aspects of consciousness.

So, it's a beautiful beginning for this day, for today we will cover what I call the light body exercise. A more noble expression for it would be "cultivating the light body."

I, Althar, have been around since the very beginning, just as you. I've seen a lot. I've seen a lot of approaches that humans took along their existence trying to overcome separation. Most often, it wasn't "pure," they did not have a *full* understanding of what separation really is. So often they did this in the face of some god who they thought existed outside of them, they wanted to please or worship him, thus they had to do certain things, but there was always that god outside. Or they were in some cult, or tribe, or spiritual order and wanted to gain certain powers, magical powers, clairvoyance, even domination over other people. There were very few exceptions like, say, the Buddha. He did not seek any power.

But there weren't too many groups in the history of this planet that where pure. And in that respect what we're doing here is really epochal. Here, we have a handful of humans – not just gathered here in this place, but also those listening in at a later time – they are not here in search for the god outside, but they are here to embody the god within.

When I feel into you, I do not feel anybody trying to do this to gain power in any way, over any other being, to embellish himself, to get riches or whatever, or to fulfill some wicked desire, no. It is just for you have seen clearly that separation is what it is – it's a constant repetition and that's against your nature. It's time to get beyond that and, well, that's why you want to embody your Godself. Godself might sound like a big, big term, but that's just accurate.

So, I scanned all the traditions, all the various approaches that humans have taken, and there's one thing in common: Those who went very deep into the mysteries, into the non-expressible, they developed a scheme of initiations, where it would take years and decades for an adapt to prepare before he would finally permitted to receive the highest teachings. Why is that?

Well, you could always say, that it's a kind of power play and those in charge pretended that they knew something special even though they didn't. True to a degree, yes, but there's another truth to it. The fact is that the highest truths are the most simple. And if you're not ready to accept the most simple truth, what happens? You will dismiss it. And when you dismiss it, it will not get a second chance in this lifetime of yours. That's what happens most of the time. And it's a pity.

So, those who are aware of, say, the highest truth, they should be very careful with voicing it, for they have a kind of responsibility. Well, it's not that they are literally responsible for another person and for what he or she chooses to do with it, but having been in separation, they should know the likelihood and probabilities of what that person is probably going to do with the teaching.

So, if you run around and tell the highest truth to whoever you meet on the street, even if the person appears to be interested, then, if it's too early for that person to fathom the truth, it will most likely be dismissed. And for what reason would you want that? It doesn't serve any purpose.

There is another thing that you might do, which is *planting the seeds*. Planting the seeds. But even this is difficult when it comes to the highest truth. Sometimes it works, sometimes not. In the end, it's not in your hand and it will never be. It's always the choice of those listening to you, what they are going to do with the wisdom. But as... well, as a teacher even without teaching, you have a certain responsibility as to what you'll bring into the world and what you present to others. So you will most likely always choose to speak in the language that those who ask can get, that helps to liberate them, and that is not prone to be dismissed too easily.

The light body exercise falls precisely in this category. The interesting thing is, all that we did in preparing for this, even yesterday, when we spoke once again about all of separation, the various realms, the various ways you have existed, previous lifetimes, future lifetimes, epochs and all the rest of that – all of this is interesting and it helps you to cope with your own memories that you might have and need to integrate into your overall life approach. But in the end, nothing of that is of *real* relevance, because you have to let it go anyway.

Because you have had so many lifetimes, it is sometimes easier to let them go if you know what they are, otherwise they are just wafting up from the unconscious and infiltrating you constantly without you even noticing it. So in that respect, it is very helpful to talk about that. But in essence, it is not necessary, it's not a requirement.

The light body exercise that we are going to do has a context, the context of compression and hypnosis. If you follow the explanation that I will give to you, you will see in detail why it works. It is even logical, it is like a recipe. Here's the diagnosis, this is what has happened and therefore you can apply this remedy. But all the background information is not really required. You could just do the light body exercise without any background information and you would end up in full enlightenment – no doubt about that.

But empirically, that's not the way it goes. That's the theory, and in theory everybody could let go of everything in any instant. However, it seldomly happens that way. So we had to have all the preparation and all the books to finally come to the most simple thing of all – to what I call cultivating your light body.

When Uru compressed you, compressed your consciousness, there was an effect that set in. I call this effect *veiling*. With the veiling you lost your natural ability to be aware of All-That-Is in separation. It's a *natural* ability and with the veiling resulting from the compression, you lost it. The more you got compressed the more you lost that ability.

Now, from those who have gone to the highest compression possible, like you have done – as you're sitting here – only very few are aware of their true nature. Your true nature has not gone, the sun has not vanished, it is where it always has been, it hasn't moved a bit. But as a result of the compression, you entered into a kind of your own consciousness bubble and lost your natural ability to be aware of your pure consciousness and of its various aspects. After the compression, there was little left within you – just small remembrances – and from there, you have started life in physicality the way you know it through thousands of incarnations, literally, until you ended up in this workshop.

The light body exercise serves many purposes and I need to mention one right now. I call this purpose the *desensitizing*. Yesterday, I mentioned briefly Uriel and the *intensity* of Uriel, because he remained so close to pure consciousness. If a human approaches pure consciousness, his own pure consciousness... Whoa, it is *so* intense that from a *human* perspective, looking through all this density and still existing veils, it is overwhelming. It's like staring into the sun. *You don't do that!* You turn your eyes away, for you do not want to get blinded. It is the very same with your pure consciousness. It's not by accident that I've chosen the metaphor of an atomic explosion, even a series of atomic explosions. You do not want to look into an atomic explosion. It would wipe you out. It is *so* strong, so far beyond what a human can imagine. Thus, you have to get desensitized and this is what the light body exercise does, besides many other things.

If a human is not prepared and for whatever reason suddenly comes across or very close to the intensity of pure consciousness, he shies away. But he felt the truth in it and then he calls it a god, or Jesus, or Krishna, or whatever term he might prefer. Something *outside* of him. "That's not me. It is so grand, it cannot be me." And – *Boom!* – here we have all the religions. "Let's do something to repeat that experience, hallelujah!" And you will never arrive there. Instead, you get all the corruption. The experts emerge knowing precisely how to serve that god outside. Even though the beginnings of a religion might have been honest and sincere, starting with the founders who might have had genuine experiences, soon, one, two generations later, we have the administrators administering the pseudo knowingness of how to do it, when in essence it's just about letting go. But there is no intermediary required and certainly no priest, no ritual, no nothing. All of that might help temporarily as a crutch, yes, but it's not required per se.

The light body exercise helps you to desensitize yourself to be able to approach that intensity of yourself. To support that, I introduced that small helpful gadget called "dimmer" that we will use when we do the exercise shortly. Dimmer, meaning a device that you imagine and that you can turn up a notch and whatever feeling we're dealing with will be intensified by, say, a factor of ten. So, turning that dimmer one notch gives you a tenfold intensity. Turning it another notch – again a tenfold intensity, another notch – tenfold, which makes it thousand times the intensity that you had in the beginning. This is the dimmer.

When the compression started and continued, and continued, and continued the veiling set in and got stronger. The veiling diminished what I denote as the *natural feeling* that you as a human have when you are within your pure consciousness. I call that feeling *bliss*, you can call it anything you want, but for our discussion here, I will call it bliss.

Bliss is the sum total of all pleasant feelings a human can ever have. The sum total. Everything is included in bliss, in its essence, in its purity, in its highest intensity. It's like the white light that you can split into various colors, red, green, blue, and all the rest of that. You can experience those individually, but when you bring them all together, you have the white light. That's the metaphor I use for bliss and what happens when parts of it are veiled, meaning you lose your natural ability to be aware of those parts.

There are three feelings I will point out specifically for the light body exercise, because they correspond to the various layers of your physical and energetic bodies. You can deal with many more layers, but there's no need to. We will just go with these three and won't get in any way technical or too detailed.

First, of course, we have the physical body. The physical body wants one thing – it wants *safety*.

Then we have the emotional body. The emotional body came into existence, because you were craving *love*, but you didn't get it, so you're craving conditional acceptance instead. That's what the emotional body is about and feeds on.

And then you have the mental body. The mental body wants *clarity*.

So, we have three feelings that correspond to three layers of your incarnated being. Back then, when the entities first incarnated, we did not know about any of these concepts. When *you* incarnated, you didn't know about bliss, you didn't know even about clarity, or safety, or love. No, you didn't know, you were in a kind of blissful state, even though you were in separation, but close, very close to pure consciousness, not that far away from it. But then you ended up here and the moment something is lacking, then you notice, "Oops – something has changed." Not only are your perception devices, your senses, restricted to a very, very narrow bandwidth, but suddenly you are lacking some very natural feelings, some natural components of you. And what do you do if you are lacking something? You try to compensate – you do it to this very day

So, if you are lacking safety, you try to compensate for safety. Now, unfortunately there's a fine print to the excursion into separation, and this fine print reads: "Listen, whatever you do in separation is bound to be made out of separation." You might say, that's the *only* rule you have in separation. Everything else follows from exactly that rule. Separation expresses itself only by means separation.

So if you have any lack of whatever kind and you try to compensate it by means of separation, well, you know what happens – *nothing* is permanent within separation, so your compensation is bound to decay.

Hence, even though you might feel a certain satisfaction for a moment, sooner or later, the reasons that gave you that feeling of satisfaction will fade away and then there's again lack. So what do you have to do? Well, you have to repeat the exercise. But even here you have a kind of desensitizing. The dose you need for the next satisfaction needs to be bigger, you all know that. That's why enough is never enough. Not only because it fades away, but because the next dose needs to be bigger.

That's why companies always want to grow, that's why the dictators want more lands around them. That's the way it is. And everybody is the same in that respect. Well, you might be at the levers of power and want to have more atomic bombs at your disposal, or you might just be in your family and you want more control over your family members. It's always the same, the same principle – enough is not enough. And even if you had a good day, tomorrow you have to repeat the same exercise.

So, we have these three layers. Let's start with the most important one that is responsible for, I would say, most of the actions of humans living in the western society who have actually no real fear for their survival. They have enough to eat, they have shelter. So then, what do they lack? Well, acknowledgement, love, and all the rest of that, what brings us to the emotional body. What you're lacking here is essentially the feeling of love. But love is an interesting thing. It is quite similar to enlightenment. *Love and separation cannot coexist.* They *cannot* coexist. Only if the borders between you and, say, another person – or it can even be a pet or whatever – are lifted, only if you let down all the guards, if you meet from true self to true self, like you did yesterday, then suddenly there's a recognition and you might call it love. There is such a deep bond. And if then some biological parameters even match, then you call it love. It's the absence of borders between you and the other. But the absence of borders is nothing else than the absence of separation.

However, as you've learned, when you are outside of separation, when you have your moments of enlightenment, at some point you are just pulled back into limitation, pulled back into your body, pulled back into physicality and all that comes with it. Then, suddenly all the boundaries are back and love is gone. Love cannot exist within separation. But the *memory* of it persists, and then you want to repeat that same feeling. Thus, you cling to the person because you had a feeling of love, so it must be a special person, right? So you do all kinds of tricks in the *hope* to repeat the experience of love.

Actually, it's not difficult to do that. Just let go of all your guards, let go of your expectations and you are beyond separation. Then, love is *everywhere*. But as you know, it's not *that* easy.

Thus, what do humans do? They settle for a cheap replacement. In their frenzied attempt to get love from somewhere. You, as a human, create all kinds of false identities that try to achieve it, by pretending to be someone, by showing a certain facade to someone from whom you think the person will like that facade, so that it might love you, which it doesn't do, because there is this facade. But at least you might get some acknowledgement. I call that *conditional acceptance*. Instead of unconditional love, you are already very happy if there is somebody who *accepts* a facade of you – conditional acceptance.

But even that fades away, so you need the next dose the next day. One day, someone you meet is nice to you, gives you a morning smile and you are happy. Life is good! The next day, he is scowling at you, you don't know why, but you might take it personally, "Oh, he has something against me, what is it?" Conditional acceptance. It's never enough.

And because this is the most pressing need a human has, this is all he does most of the time. Pampering his facade in the hope that others might like it. And it might be enough if there is just one who likes it. That's better than nothing. But true love? Be honest with yourself. Yes, you *hope* for it, but for how many *seconds* have you experienced it in your life? How many seconds? Maybe just as long as you have experienced true enlightenment, being beyond separation.

So that's the nature of living in separation. You lack something, you want to compensate for it.

Then we have clarity. Clarity and the mental body. Oh, the mental body is huge, it's truly huge. When the compression set in, doubts came. In pure consciousness, you have no questions, thus you do not doubt. Whereas in separation, there are only questions. In separation, there was never a single answer that did not raise another ten questions. With very few exceptions, like maybe in mathematics, where you have dead made-up things that are not alive. You can say, well, the circumference of a square is like that. Okay, cool. But it's dead.

Everything that has consciousness to it, that has life to it, well, that just raises questions. Every answer is just preliminary. And look at your experts and scientists, they change their opinions every decade at least. What was wrong yesterday is hyped today and tomorrow it's replaced by something else. Why is that if it was science?

Well, it is because it's based on perception and perception is always false. It's colored by your past, by your hopes, by your fears, by your desires. Even if you pretend to search for the truth, you still want to be *acknowledged* by your colleagues. So you better don't say something that you know your colleagues will dismiss. They will kill you, not with stones these days, but they will not cite you, for instance, if you are a physicist or something comparable. And that's your scientific death, because you need that in the world of science. So you have to comply. You create another facade, you compromise on the truth.

So, where has clarity gone? Well, it doesn't exist in separation. And you know that instantly and intuitively. Thus, what do you do? You try to replace it or compensate it with *control*. Because if there is a controlled environment, then you know what is going to happen. Then you know the outcome and can *pretend* there's clarity.

If you live in a small prison cell, then everything is pretty much controlled. There's not much surprise and you might feel like the king in your prison cell, and you are, to a degree. Whatever happens, you know the response in advance. That's control. But it's not clarity and it's certainly not freedom. It does not befit a creator being.

Still, that's the way people do it. They want to control everything and even if they are on a spiritual quest, they want to control the outcome of it. "Oh, I want to let go of everything, but today I have something to do, I have an important appointment. Tomorrow might be better to do that." They want to control. They might want to change, but if the change is coming, "Oops, huh! That might be too much, I have to control it." That's the way it is and I don't blame anybody for that, for me, Althar, being a non-physical being, I cannot even imagine how it is to be in a physical body. No one on our side can, unless they have been incarnated. And that's the reason why everybody on this side is so in awe of what you're doing. So even if I state the truth about separation and the way the humans function in it, it is not to belittle you in any way. It is just about clarifying the patterns you are following and the reasons *why* you follow these patterns. By becoming aware of them, you might choose to let them go.

A human can live without clarity, and he can live without love, as you see when you look around. People live their lives somehow, some of them pretend to be happy. But a human cannot live without safety. You cannot compensate for it in any significant manner. You can compensate for love or you tell yourself you don't need it, because you love yourself. Okay, if you believe that, fine.

You can compensate for clarity by controlling your environment and say, "Well, that's enough for me, I don't need anymore, I'm fine." But safety? Safety is a difficult one, for by being in a physical body you know that you will die. And no matter what you do in this lifetime, no matter what mountains you will move, no matter how much power or non-power you have, death will be the end of your incarnation, just as it was in all of your previous lifetimes. Death *will* come and you *know* it.

It's interesting that people continue enjoying certain things because they know, "Oh, my life has an end, so I better enjoy this ice cream." And why shouldn't they? But, this is not really the way of living for a creator being. A creator being would say, "Well, I was not even born, so why not enjoy this ice cream. (laughs) If I wasn't born, why would I die?"

So, safety cannot be compensated for. This knowingness is innate, it's everywhere, it's deep down in every cell of yours, no matter how big the castles and walls are that you build around you, be they of money, or knowledge, or power – *your body will die and you know it.*

If you are a dictator, your greatest fear is your own security guards, because they might murder you. They are allowed to come close to protect you, but so often they just kill you. Or your own family kills you, happens all the time. And you know that, so can you even enjoy all that power and wealth that you might have accumulated? No, you can't.

Safety is the biggest burden. You cannot compensate for it. Therefore, safety is the first that we approach with the light body exercise. Now, if I would tell you this out of context, if I meet you on the street and tell you, "Have you heard? There is safety and it's really important, you should become aware of the feeling of safety within you." "Yeah, sounds interesting, let me have my ice cream first." It doesn't work that way, so we have to put it in context, you have to make people *feel* the validity of it. They *really* have to feel the validity of it, then they might give it a chance and then this highest truth can unfold its whole potency. Otherwise, it is just dismissed like the wise sayings on your calendar.

Good. Let's start with the actual light body exercise. We will play some music. And then we'll go through it step by step.

(music plays)

As always, start from the physical body. Become present, take on a royal position. It is about *this* moment, not the next. Become aware of your body, for this is the temple that you live in right now. This is the temple of beauty, this is with what you interact in this world. So honor your body. It serves you. It is the embedded human consciousness that creates all the problems, the body itself is perfectly fine.

Let the breath come in and out. Allow yourself to expand. Become more and more aware. Become even aware of your awareness.

One might say that the moment you are aware of your awareness, you are one with your true self. It is not that the outside world is gone, it's just there, in a way, but it doesn't bother you. You *are*. You do not need to express yourself in any way, still you are without any need to reflect yourself.

Now, from that level of your true self, hold the intent of having a light body. Don't ask *how*, just do it and it will be there, for that is the nature of pure consciousness. Whatever it intents will be so.

From that level of your true self, imagine us being a few kilometers above Earth, looking down on the humans. Why are they doing what they're doing? Why are they *truly* doing what they're doing?

I hinted at it in my explanations. The core reason for anything they do is the desire to feel the feeling that is associated either with the outcome of what they're doing, or experienced *while* they're doing it. If there weren't the feelings, *why* would you do anything other than take care of your bare survival? It is always, always, always the feeling that you want, that the humans want. That's what they are craving.

And here, from the level of your true self, you realize that there is *no need for any outer stimulation* of whatever feelings you like to feel. The humans always try to arrange circumstances on the outside, so that those circumstances then give them the opportunity to feel something, given that their plan works out. If not, they go into depression, "I've failed once again."

But what if, what if this most, most, most simple truth in separation would be *really* a truth, *even for you?* The truth that you can become aware *from within* of any feeling that you desire, for it is a part of your natural beingness. Yes, it was veiled, but now that you know, now that you are aware of that, now that you've lifted the veil, *you can become aware within you of any feeling that you desire without having to arrange anything on the outside.*

I want you to take two minutes to feel into that. What would it mean for you, if that truth would really be *your* truth in your personal life. No need to go outside to experience a certain feeling.

*

Understanding separation is one thing. It's not that difficult to see separation for what it is. Many did and so they came up with all kinds of ways to deal with it, to walk on the sunny side of polarity as long as possible, to get in balance with Ying and Yang, knowing how the cycles work and all the rest of that. Yeah, it's fine for a while. But going beyond that is not easy.

So, I would say, apart from understanding the nature of separation, knowing about the availability of feelings from within is the one key that really helps you to let go. And you need it, because separation is so *sticky*. It sticks everywhere. Having that innate understanding that you can be aware of any feeling that you desire, *of any feeling that you desire* – that is the easiest and most direct way to set yourself free from each and every pattern that you are working out each day to get something on the outside. But it is so simple that it can easily be dismissed.

There's no *need* to have any background information. One does not even need to mention Atlantis or a dragon. This truth is so simple. Anybody could follow it today. But then, even if you felt the validity of it, still there is the unconscious of you. There's you being bound to physicality by hypnosis. There are all those cells, the consciousness within your cells, that believe they would die if you let go.

Even if the insight sets in that feelings can be created from within, you have to do it without looking for results, without crawling along a linear timeline. You do it in the moment and you free yourself in the moment.

So, now let's come back to your physical appearance and feel the light body. It's all around your body, it envelopes your physical body and your emotional body, so it's larger than your physical appearance. It is all around you, and it even penetrates you, it is everywhere within you. It's even in the space between the space. It's between the atoms and cells, even in between your thoughts, it's everywhere. That's your light body.

Now bring forth the feeling of safety. And when I say "bring forth" I do not mean that you create it. You never create any feeling, you never did. Whenever you have a feeling, you are just opening up to a feeling that is already there. That's all that happens. So, when I say "bring forth" I mean *open up* to the feeling of safety that is within your light body. Feel safe.

Sometimes it's easier to single out a feeling by to starting with its opposite. You most certainly had instances in your life where you felt completely *unsafe*. Like in an airplane, or maybe you have experienced an earthquake, anything when you felt completely out of control and your life was threatened. You've felt quite unsafe. Now, as we sit here, it's relatively safe. Feel the difference. Right now, nothing threatens your life. And then let go of the memories and stay with that feeling of safety.

Your body is safe. Each and every cell is safe. You do not have to defend anything. You can let go of all guards, of your armor. No need to fight, no need to pretend even, for you are safe. Nothing can harm you.

Now, take that dimmer and turn it up one notch. Intensify the feeling of safety multiplied by a factor of ten. That's way more than you're used to. Allow that to happen, you have support from many sides here. You are already in safety now.

A human doesn't know safety. He doesn't. Can you imagine going somewhere *feeling safe?* Nobody can harm you, *nobody* can harm you, because you know you are within a dream and you are a lucid dreamer, so to speak. Even an illness cannot harm you, for *you are not your body!* You're not. You're a free being. And right now, in this very moment, you are safe, you are unborn, there's no death.

Once again, take that dimmer, safety times ten.

You might feel the tingling in your body. Finally, finally the consciousness embedded in your body can relax. Did it *ever* relax? Has it ever? Oh, yes, in the moments of death, but those were very short.

See, you do nothing. This is the true practice – you just become aware of what already is.

Once again, take the dimmer. Current safety times ten, which is a thousand times more intense than we had in the beginning.

Bath in that feeling, it's like a warm embrace. In a way, this is how the non-physical entities feel, for they do not fear death. And by doing the light body exercise, we are approaching your pure consciousness.

Specifically, when you do this alone, when there's not so much talk, you can really dive into it. Then you will feel how so much from the unconscious is be boiled up. It will come to the forefront. It will get highlighted, in a way, for its – how to say – living conditions suddenly change. There's light where it used to be dark. But you see, the sun doesn't care if there's a dog barking at it or a shadow is running around. Sun doesn't care. And you know what? That is the greatest compassion of all. In this dream, there is nothing you have to pity or rescue. Actually, whatever was in that dream never *really* happened. Isn't that the nature of dreams?

By going a thousand times stronger you desensitize yourself. You cannot survive as an enlightened being on Earth in mass consciousness, amongst so many, huh, so many limited people. I almost said zombies or living dead, but that's not accurate, they are on their way, it wouldn't be too compassionate to term them that way. But it's difficult to live amongst them. Therefore, it's not enough if you're just a little bit "beyond" them. You have to be *fully* out of this world, then you can be here without getting harmed and without being sucked back.

Next. Keep that feeling of safety. And now we go to love. Remember a moment of love you have had in this lifetime. Just one moment. Be it your first romantic love, your current love, or it might even be an occasion with a pet, with something innocent. That feeling of "no boundaries", but still there is another entity accepting you as you are, not challenging you.

Now, let go of that memory and stay with the feeling. You are safe and there's love. Wow! A love that is not directed to anything. It's just there, it's within you. It's not coming from the outside. You can *feel* it. That's unusual for most humans.

Use your dimmer and intensify the love by a factor of ten. Again, the feeling is already there, you just allow yourself to become aware of it. You let go of that veil, for now you have matured, you allow yourself to do that, to be so bold and go way, way, way beyond the typical bandwidth of a human, without shying back, without being over-whelmed by the intensity.

Once again, take your dimmer – love times ten.

It's everywhere within you. A gentle caress, a loving touch from you for you. And it's not limited to you. Actually, it is everywhere. If you are in love with yourself, if you feel the love within yourself, well, there's love everywhere. That's just the way it is, if there's no separation.

For the last time, take the dimmer – love times ten. Intensify! Go way beyond what's normal, what you've allowed yourself up to this point. Do not limit your love, do not try to radiate it, but become aware that it's actually everywhere.

A human in love, being safe. Can you remember when you've been in love? You remember the fear you had that love would go away? That was the price of love – the fear it might vanish. Feeling unsafe in your love. But now, without doing anything, suddenly here we are in a human body, absolutely safe and overflowing with love. Without any outer conditions.

In a way, we are approaching the white light.

Once again, a hint. When you do this alone in the future – and I urge you to do it regularly, for it's the most beautiful thing you can do to yourself – you will often feel heavy reactions in your physical body. Emotions coming up, tears, fears, sometimes anger. Try not to get distracted by them. And do not even think, "Ah, yes, it's working, now I got it!" It *does* work. And when those reactions occur, just allow them, just allow them. Do not follow them.

Take your time. No need to rush anything. That's the wisdom that you need, the discernment. Do not push, even though we are pushing. Do not desire, even through we are desiring. That's the paradox that you have to live with. But you desire the highest and you do it without doing. Still, because you have been so long in separation, it has side effects that you have to be able to cope with. So, take your time and enjoy the ride.

Now clarity. Oh, the clarity. Humans have gotten so mental, *so* mental. With mental I do not mean the precise scientific thoughts which are very helpful if you want to understand separation. It is perfectly fine to use the mind like that. But with mental I mean churning your thoughts, going in circles, thinking about emotions, thinking, trying to predict what a person might do, or not do, or why someone has done something and why have you failed again. That is what I mean by mental – trying to come up with an answer for a question, knowing that you can never solve or implement it anyway. This is frustrating, so you try to find another solution by staying in the mental, and thus you move in circles.

But true clarity means *you know that you know*. You know who you are. You simply know, *I am that I am.* That is clarity. *That* is clarity. Clarity is not the product of a sophisticated mind, it's a letting go and becoming aware of that clarity.

You might picture your mental content that you have as a firmament of stars in the sky, *numerous* thoughts, ideas, convictions, beliefs, theories, concepts. And even they fight for survival, because they want your awareness, of course. Otherwise, how could they sustain their lives? They are radiating at all times, "Look at me, look at me. Give me your awareness for awareness is life." What else would life be other than giving awareness to anything?

Now, let that clarity flow in. Maybe for the first time in your life, in all of your lives, you might encounter what it means to relax in the mental body.

Let the *concepts* relax.

There *is* clarity, there's no need to *fabricate* it. You might even pair the clarity with love and safety.

So many ideas and concepts are like sharp knives. They are just there to cut, to separate right and wrong, to create dogma. They dictate your life, they attempt to control your life so you can feel safe. What a poor, poor way of being. Now, let all that relax. The sky itself resembles the clarity. It's not its content, it's not the stars, not the clouds. And the sky is not holding on to those stars and clouds. They might be bright or dark, even a dark hole, a black hole – sky doesn't care, it just remains being sky. "So what? I am in clarity."

Now, clarity times ten. And you might feel the magnitude of your mental body – it's huge. It's *huge*.

Once again, clarity times ten. "I know that I know. I'm pure consciousness. I'm not bound to whatever I perceive. I am not a product of separation and most certainly, I do not have to clean up separation."

There's no need to create any kind of happy ending to your dream. You can just let go.

Once again, clarity times ten. Let's go intense. The brightest light that ever walked on planet

Earth. By really going out of your personal comfort zone, at some point you will really realize how the doubt just puffs away. It knows, it truly does, that nothing, nothing, nothing can stand pure consciousness. It surrenders, it gives up. Pfff – if puffs away. You do not care anymore for the doubt, for it was you who gave life to the doubt.

These three feelings cover pretty much the spectrum that determine your actions as an incarnated human. But now let's bring in more feelings.

We start with my favorite – beauty. Oh, beauty. Feel beauty. A beautiful symphony, beautiful music, a beautiful sunset, a sculpture, literature, dance. Any beautiful expression. But you know what? It is not the *expression* that creates beauty, not at all. It *reminds* you of the beauty, it's a *reminder*. And because of that are these expressions so valuable. But they do not contain the beauty. They remind you of your innate beauty, they nudge you to remember it, to open up to it. So, without any outer stimulus become aware of beauty.

When you are in beauty, time stands still. It is said that your heart stops beating, it skips a beat. That's what beauty does – you are in shock, you are in awe. "My god! How can *that* exist? It is *so* beautiful!" You literally stop aging in that moment, for time stands still. And the beauty has always been with you, always.

Now, beauty times ten. And times ten, and times ten. This is beauty times a thousand. Combined with all the other feelings, we are approaching bliss here.

When you are on your own, feel free to take any feeling of your liking and add it. Joy. Peace. Contentedness. Freedom. Serenity. There are so many beautiful aspects of bliss. Bring them all in. Intensify them.

Now, let's get a bit symbolic with bliss. You might have noticed that I've abstained from all kinds of body work, such as you have in so many other teachings. I'm not talking about chakras, merkabas, or anything like that, I'm not technical at all. Yes, we could, but in the end, as we have seen so often, you always end up with trying to perfect your human body, trying to have the best spinning chakras with as many petals as you like. All this leads you astray, nowhere. Ultimately, you need to let go of it anyway. There's only one exception I make, and that's with bliss, so that it can be felt more easily.

Place your awareness fifteen centimeters above your head.

See, it's so easy. Why is it easy? Because you have no center, there's no center anywhere in existence. Place your awareness fifteen centimeters above your head and then feel safety, love, clarity, beauty up there, with the utmost intensity. Throw away the dimmer and go all in.

The brightest light you've ever seen. But luckily, you do not need your physical senses to become aware of it. They would be burned away. You need no sense to be aware of who you truly are, for *you are you*. And the natural feeling of you, from a human perspective, is bliss. You can even call it true self. True self is very close. Even though you picture it above your head, it doesn't mean a true self enters separation the way you do. But still, it's so close, maybe it has never been closer to you.

Now, allow that sphere of white light, with the size of an orange, to sink slowly, slowly into your skull. It's loving, it's bright, it's safe. It is *you*.

The light penetrates your physical senses. You might say, it washes away the distortions from the eyes, from your thoughts. It strips off your associations with the past, for did things really happen the way you think they did?

Let it sink deeper. Oh, the light remains in the head, but the sphere of bliss, the true self, sinks deeper. Through your throat. It touches your throat.

Imagine, each word you utter, would be touched and filled with the bliss of yourself. Not wanting anything, not needing anything, not pitying anything. What a blessing for all those who come in touch with you. No sermons. No rituals. Just a single word of you, a glance with the eyes and all is said, all is said.

Now let the sphere sink deeper to the center of your chest. Let it touch your heart. Humans equate the heart with the center of love. So be it, I don't care. Feel it there – *bliss*. It contains all the love that exists. It was never gone. It accepts you as you are. It comes with safety, with knowingness. It is *eternal*. It has no precondition, no cause, therefore it will not vanish.

Let it fill your chest and then let it sink deeper into your belly, into the spot below your navel, down to the center of your belly.

Huh, can you feel the safety that radiates from there?

Words might be nice, but when you suddenly *feel* the truth of it, oh, then all changes. Even if you think that you have understood and accepted something, the moment you *feel* it, it changes *totally* its character. And you would not want to talk about it to just anybody. They need to be ready, so they don't dismiss it.

Feel that utmost safety right in the belly of yours. Let the sphere of bliss, of your true self, expand. Let it grow from there. It did meld with the light body that is already there. Actually, it is the light body.

A loving embrace on all levels of your existence. Why would you need any false identities trying to get something if everything was already there? Just allow yourself to become aware of it at any time.

Let that bliss grow and grow and grow. Take note! You are sitting here with a few other humans, and all of them are boundless. At the same time, you can *feel* them. They still exist. They are just as unlimited as you are. You are not different, still you are sovereign. That's nothing a human can ever comprehend. But you can feel it.

You can feel it and please, take note of this feeling. You are not alone in this journey. You have never been. You have never been alone in this journey. In a few days, it might occur to you that all you have experienced in this gathering was just a dream within a dream, but it wasn't. The mind will come in and make it smaller and smaller, packaging it into a small thought. Don't allow that.

If there is no separation, where does the inside end and the outside begin?

Expand. Allow your light body and your true self having joined with you. This is the living trinity. Allow it to expand to the All-That-Is for it was never restricted.

*

Separation? Really?

*

This is a moment of embodied ascension. Just as there are moments of enlightenment and moments of love, there are moments of embodied ascension, and this is one of them. It's in the now, it's not tomorrow.

Can you feel it? You have a physical body, you are one with your true self, and you have let go of separation – that is the dream come true.

*

Allow this experience, this wisdom, this simplicity to take deep roots within the Third Round of Creation. Existence beyond separation. You have access to both, separation and the Third Round of Creation.

In the first book I've introduced myself as being a "bridge in consciousness." And so are you.

Can you allow it to be *so simple?* Simple. It's not even an exercise, that's why I called it "cultivating" the light body. Applying a *single* insight – humans lack feelings. Okay, give them the feelings and they can go beyond being human. It's two sentences. But only the most mature beings are ready to understand it, accept it, and put it into practice.

There's no reason to leave this expanded state, this expanded nature of you. You still have a human body with certain desires and pulls coming from there, but do not fear falling out of this state, for you have access to it anytime you want, and you can be there *instantly*.

Go moment by moment. Moment by moment. The benefits of this simple, simple "cultivation of your light body" with regards to your physical body, your emotional body, and your mental body cannot be described in words. They all *relax*. The fight vanishes. But do not do it to cure an illness or even an aspect. Just go beyond that and allow those things to happen naturally in time. You yourself though are beyond time.

The music will play five more minutes of linear time and then we will have a break, if you so choose, or you might just stay in this expanded consciousness forever.

I am Althar. I'm meeting you again soon.

4. The Field of Consciousness Experiment

In this session, we'll start where we left off in the previous session, the light body, and then we will do an experiment.

I will play some music and in the next five minutes bring forth your light body. All on your own without the words. Then, Althar will join us and we'll continue from there.

* * *

(Music plays)

*

I am Althar, the Crystal Dragon!

You heard me admit that I am a lover of beauty, and the greatest beauty that I'm aware of is when consciousness opens up, when illusions are illuminated and just dissolve. In such an instant, there is kind of a fireworks taking place, a sublime light is emitted. What we have witnessed in the previous session from the other side is unparalleled true beauty. Pure consciousness, unmasking separation, freeing itself. That is the joy of those who choose to stay after their enlightenment. At least it is my joy when observing you from the other side. It might also be your joy should you choose to stay. Oh, there are other joys that you might experience, but this is my finest pleasure.

Unfortunately, nothing is easy in separation and this also holds for bliss. So I have to make two, three cautionary notes concerning bliss. The first is, whenever you experience something like we just did in the previous session, then of course you want to repeat it. Then, what often happens is, a human goes into his memories and replays the movie of his experiences. But of course this is not the same as enacting it afresh. So be very aware of what you are doing when you attempt to go into bliss in a given now moment. Are you just replaying a movie, a nice scene from the past, or is it real?

Do not try to fabricate it. Allow it to happen. It happens by letting go, by allowing yourself to become aware of what is already there. Once in a while though, the circumstances are difficult. There are so many influences around you, here in polarity, that sometimes it just does not work out. When you feel that, then don't be disappointed. That's when you need true compassion, knowing that you know about true reality, even though for whatever reason, you cannot realize it in the moment. But *never* try to enforce it, this will always work against you.

Just be content even if you cannot get "out there" and have the same depth of feelings as you might have had in the previous session. At such a point, it is always good to cultivate your awareness. Just be aware of what is there, annoying feelings, annoying emotions, annoying anger – just let them pass away. The sun is always there and if you do not push then at some point the sun will become openly available for you once again.

Once you have entered bliss, as we have done before, then there might be a symptom that I call "post bliss depression." Post bliss depression, for you have felt from a human perspective the most sublime that exists and then you come back into the harsh physical reality, enter the next bus to go to work, and suddenly you are crushed by everything that is all around you.

It's not easy to deal with that. You see all these limited humans, craving attention, craving power, and you remember the bliss where you just came from and ask yourself, "Why the heck am I back here? Wouldn't it be great if this bliss stayed with me at al times?" But don't go there! If you realize you are in post bliss depression, take advantage of separation by knowing that nothing in separation lasts. So even that depression will fade. That's just the way it is. Nothing is only good nor bad.

Once the chemicals are floating in your body, it's not that easy to step out of what they are doing to your feelings and emotions. So you just observe, be aware. Yes, depression does not feel good, but do not try to fight it, you cannot push it away, you would only make it more real – and it is not *that* real.

The other cautionary note relates to a state that is severe although it sounds a bit funny. I call it the "bliss junky." A bliss junky is like a normal junky who is on drugs and needs his next shot, because he cannot deal with daily life, with physical reality. He has to run away, he has to go into his own bubble of drug-induced well-being. Bliss could become a drug quite easily. Nothing in the physical world can compete with bliss, but don't go there. *Don't go there!* Bliss is not an escape, it's your natural state. If you intend to stay incarnated you need to be *aware* at all times even when entering bliss.

Going into bliss *without* being aware is similar to what you call the deep sleep. There is *nothing* going on, no perception, no dreams. The body relaxes, but all the rest stays the same. The unconscious stays the same. The impulses and patterns remain. If you go unaware into bliss and just let yourself float around there, then you have no chance to make embodied ascension a reality for you. You're just an addict. You're addicted to a certain feeling that you can "create" within yourself, which might be better than using chemicals, but other than that there is not much of a difference.

When you are aware while you are in bliss, meaning you *see* separation for what it really is, then all the patterns, all the emotional stimuli that you have, run out of momentum. The momentum gets less and then ceases. This is what eventually will set you free.

So, post bliss depression and the bliss junky – be aware of those. It's not that difficult, just be aware of them. Don't go there or be prepared and let them go.

Now, let's do an experiment and for that I ask you, please, to get closer. We have an empty chair in the center and so please adjust your chairs in order to create a tight circle.

We'll repeat the light body exercise from the previous session, everybody on his or her own, but now we create a... what's the best term... a consciousness field by means of our light bodies. We connect our light bodies and by doing so, a, huh, "Buddha field" is created in the center, a Buddha field. When you do the light body exercise on your own and go into high intensity, then this is already huge. But when several embodied beings come together and do it simultaneously, then a huge synergy sets in. It is not just that the intensities are added, they are multiplied.

So, first be aware of your light body and let it grow such that it envelopes the whole group. All of you do it simultaneously. No need to protect anything. You know you are safe and all the rest of that.

You might currently have a very precious sensation. Being in your pure consciousness, fully aware, in your sovereign domain, yet you are together with other human beings who are in their very own sovereign domain – it's a shared dream. Each one of you is sovereign, absolutely free to react in whatever way he or she wants. Thus, when your light bodies overlap, there is no *need* to react. They are all similar to yours, but still each entity's light body has a certain characteristic stemming from all the experiences that entity had in separation. Those are typically different from yours, although not *that* different.

So, quickly become aware of safety, let it spread out, of love that is just there and let it spread out, of clarity and of bliss. Use the dimmer to intensify it while feeling the others all around you.

*

We did the true encounter in the first session. Now you can feel that you can have the very same encounter even with closed eyes – you can feel them just the same.

The unconscious is grand, it's huge. Bringing light into the unconscious... what's the best way to express it... makes it dissolve, lets the impulses and memories revert to pure consciousness serving you in your expression. If you do the light body exercise on your own, it is already very intense, but what do you think might happen if you take a seat in the center of this combined light body? Surrounded by friends of old, kindred spirits, sharing the same dream of enlightenment and embodiment. Surrounded by full acceptance, *full acceptance*. No need to pretend anything, for everybody here knows all the pitfalls, all the ups and downs.

So, just sit in that center spot, letting go of your guards, eyes closed – we will just go into the feelings. If anybody is brave and wants to experience this, well, take that seat in the center.

(someone takes place in the center)

It's a spot where you cannot hide anything and where you do not *want* to hide anything – this is a blessing.

Feel all that you are, all that you have been, all of your journey – it's a review, a full acceptance. It's a forgiveness. The true forgiveness is to realize that nothing that seemingly happened actually ever did happen. It's a dream. Remnants of dreams. Visits of already existing scene spheres of separation. No need to clean up anything.

In such a moment you can notice that it is really not about you. It is not about your personal history. It not even about the human who is incarnated in this very moment.

This is about the totality of your true self and all its experiences.

You might rotate with the chair and feel how it is to sense the others from the back and the front.

Take your time.

You in the outer circle, be simultaneously in your physical body, feel from there *and* feel from the level of your true self. You might envision this as being high above this room, a kilometer or so. See the grander picture and see the details. It's a celebration, a dream come true, being amongst friends.

You might change to the next one, whoever is ready to take that seat.

(several changes in the center)

* * *

(Joachim now sits in the center)

Some of you might have felt, while sitting in the center, the dragons being all around us. Typically, I do not speak much about the dragons even though I am a dragon, simply not to distract you with other creatures. But the dragons are here. Many of them. They have been right here in the center, they're companions since a long time.

A dragon embodies – without having a physical body – clarity and compassion, and they come in to assist you in your true practice.

Now I, Althar, will make myself very, very present here in the center and invite all of you to become aware of the clarity and compassion that is within you. Then, if you so choose, a dragon will join you to accompany you in your journey.

*

You are not alone in this journey. You have never been, even though you might have felt like that.

Preparation is over. It's time to get real.

As a human, you have only one choice of importance. What do you choose? The Eye of Suchness or the Eye of Separation?

Let the dragon remind you of that choice over and over again, the best friend you'll ever have. He's beyond time, or she's beyond time – just as you like to see it.

The dragon has no agenda. It's just a loving reminder of who you truly are. A bridge in consciousness, so to speak.

To end the session, I invite you all to stand up and make that gesture of gratitude (Gassho/Namaste). Thanks to all of you for being here, for being who you are.

The music will continue to play if you want to stay and let that energy sink in. That's up to you.

I am Althar, the Crystal Dragon. It was once again a great honor for me to be with you.

5. Althar, the Atlantean

I am Althar, the Atlantean.

It's once again a delight for me to be with you. It is my third appearance in a workshop setting. I had my first appearance in the very first workshop that Joachim did, and back then I didn't feel very comfortable. I told a little bit of my story. Then I was persuaded to come in again just three weeks ago to share an important detail of my story that is very important to you as you go further into your embodied ascension. So, now this is my third time coming into a workshop. I still feel a bit reluctant. I like to stay more in the background, for my history, my personal history, still weighs a bit on me.

My story has been written about from the perspective of the dragon and from the perspective of my loving partner at the times, Echnatara. But now I will convey a bit of my story to you. How I, in a way, became enlightened, how I tried to spread enlightenment amongst my people, and what happened to me. The whole reason why I do this is to make you cautious. Separation is a tricky thing and you can easily fall. At no time should you be reckless or push too much.

In my day, you might say, we were naive, but we just didn't know any better. We had no experience with enlightenment and how it would get along with normal consciousness. So what does life do, what do people do if they don't know? Well, they have to go into it, do the best they can, they have to experience it, and so often they just tumble. That's just the way it is. And, in a way, that happened to me. But nothing, nothing is in vain. Not even in separation, for time is not linear and you being here, so many of your Earth years later, you can learn so much from my personal story.

My personal story is indeed not that special, really not. There have been many following a similar track, but because the dragon is here and asks me to tell it, Joachim asks me to tell it, Echnatara, in a way, pushes me from the other side to tell it also, well, then I'm here for the third time and will just do it once again.

I was born to a group, to a community, in the early times of Atlantis when the technology was just rising. I came in as a conscious birth, meaning my mother knew she was birthing me, me having been an elder of the community. I had lived there before, many lifetimes. I was to become the so called "Master of the Energies" for my community was totally dedicated to exploring the energies. Imagine a community dedicated to exploring the energies. Back then, we had no dogma, no religion, no god, nothing. We were just curious about life and exploring the energies to see how we could use them to our advantage. Well, that was our pleasure, and it served us well in our daily life.

So I was born. I came in with many of the talents I had honed in my previous lifetimes. Because the birth was conscious, I knew quite a bit of myself from back then and thus it was easy for me to relearn what I had learned in the previous lifetimes. Thus, after I had grown up, I occupied my position as the Master of Energies.

But at some point, I noticed a call from within, a question. And the question was, "Well, I'm the master of the energies, but do I have any clue what energy *is*? Where it *comes* from?" So my personal quest became, "What is the *source* of energy?" The source of energy. And it puzzled me. I became obsessed with that question. I tried to come to a solution, I tried to have my community work with me on that problem, but they simply couldn't understand the whole issue. *Why* think about something like that? There's plenty of energy everywhere, so what is the point in knowing anything about the source of energy? Why not just exploit what is there and be done with it?

But I wasn't content. I became grumpy. I didn't want to talk to the people anymore. I felt like an outsider. I wanted to pursue that question and so we came to an arrangement – me with my community – they wanted me to go off and I wanted to be off. So we arranged that I went up into the mountains, to a hut where I could do my research about the source of energy. And some nice lady would provide me food every other day, every ten days or so. So there was nothing I needed to take care for, other than for my quest.

I went to that hut and in the beginning I enjoyed it very much, for I was *alone* there. I was totally on my own, I didn't have to comply to any rules of the community. I didn't have to be polite or nice to anybody. I could just be myself without any facade.

And I started my exploration of the source of energy. I searched, and searched, and questioned, and questioned, but the only thing I could observe was a *transformation* of energy, a constant transformation of energy, but at no point was energy *created*. And that made me really depressed, for where else could I look, where else could I search? I had already searched everywhere.

But then, when I was really close to give up on that question and come back to the normal life in the community, there was an intuition. And that intuition whispered to me, "Listen, Althar, you've looked everywhere on the *outside*, but never ever did you look *within*." And that made perfect sense to me. Well, if I have looked everywhere else and didn't find it, then it must be in the place where I did not search before.

So I started looking within. You have to understand, at that point in time, regarding the development of consciousness, there wasn't a notion even for consciousness itself. It just didn't exist! And of course, there was no notion of something like introspection, looking within. That was completely new. I might have been the only one on the whole planet at that time that did something crazy like that – introspection, going within.

But anyway, I did it. And boy, was I shocked when I first consciously became aware of all the things going on within me. Thoughts! You see, even the concept of a "thought", an individual thought, wasn't really in our vocabulary. I, in a sense, discovered thoughts for myself for the very first time. Same with emotions, same with feelings, same with memories.

I sat there and looked within, I even forgot to look for energy, because I was so fascinated with everything that was going on within me. And at some point, I simply noticed, "Wow, whatever comes up, I can let go. It doesn't define me, so I am not what I can perceive." And that was, in a way, even more interesting than the whole quest for the source of energy. If I'm not what I can perceive then, what the hell, am I? Well, there might be a source of energy that I won't find, but maybe it's even a bigger pressure to find out who I am? And so I ventured deeper and deeper and deeper.

I had ideal circumstances, you see. I had no dogma in my backpack, I had no education that limited me in any way. We were a community of curiosity, of expansion, of moving forward. I didn't have to deal with bad parents or shocking experiences in my lifetime. We were nice to each other, we were not hostile, we were friendly. Other communities in the neighborhood, oh, they had a different structure, hierarchies, and they were even hostile amongst themselves. But our community? We were safe and friendly.

So I had ideal, really *ideal* circumstances to go within and just be with myself. I did not even have to take care of my food, planting plants, go begging, or anything like that. No, I was provided by a nice lady. I did not meet her at first. She always placed the food somewhere in front of the hut and when she was gone I came and picked it up.

So I went in and in and in, all on my own. At some point, I came to the place that you call *emptiness* or the void, nothing. Just nothing – the total absence of perception. But still I was. And that was, ah, a *bit* frightening, but *fascinating* at the same time.

I hear now that so many humans run away from this void, from facing this nothingness, what they feel to be an abyss, threatening them with extinction. Me personally, I was more fascinated. Yes, it might be a bit intimidating when you are in that void, but I had no fear, just no fear. Maybe that was my blessing or talent, I cannot say, but I *loved* going there. I loved just being there and when I returned, when my body called me back – it had needs, toilet needs, feeding, and such – then I noticed, how I reverted to my human mode. But still I had the remembrance of the void.

I had nobody to share this with and this is, as you have found out even in your life, not easy to deal with. Being lonely usually means not being able to share what is really important to you with somebody else. That is the definition of being lonely. You can be amongst two thousand people, but if you cannot share what is important to you, you are still lonely. In that respect, maybe I was the loneliest man on the planet at the time. I knew nobody to talk to. I couldn't even imagine going back to the community and speaking about things you now call consciousness, thoughts, going within, the void, letting go, and all the rest of that. They would not have listened, no chance.

At that point though, a good friend of me, or someone who became a good friend of mine – and meanwhile also for you – came in. At the time, I just called him "the dragon." Now he calls himself Althar, for he took my name in honoring me, but we are skipping ahead here.

At that point, I just noticed there's this presence that was known even in our times as the dragon. He wasn't physical, he came in non-physically with *full* presence, with *full* compassion. I will never forget our first encounter. It was *intense*. It was so intense that I wanted to run away, but then, at the same time, I felt a loving compassion.

In that first encounter, we had eye contact, so to speak. You might say from a human perspective, the dragon, well, he *tested* me. Could I stand his presence? For what he did was, well, he looked at me in my entirety. And whoever has been incarnated knows that in all the lifetimes you had in physical or non-physical lifeforms, you did certain things that stick to you that were not that beautiful. But the dragon saw it all and invited me to see it also. It was like all these events were lined up as a string of pearls and the dragon shed a bright light on each of them, inviting me to just look at what I didn't want to see. And I was able to do that. So, let's say, I passed the test. But still, because the intensity felt so strong in the beginning, those encounters couldn't last too long.

But from that moment on, I had a companion. A companion in my explorations of what I call the void and consciousness. That was a blessing for me. So whenever henceforth I went into introspection, when I went within and then came back, I knew the dragon would be there. Not asking anything, not even explaining anything, but me feeling his presence, I knew I was not alone.

We shared without words and that gave me so much comfort. It was what you have been doing here, the "true encounter." You just get in the presence of another being, accepting each other, no need to share anything explicitly, but the sheer acceptance is what allows an exchange on the deepest level without words. Thus you know you're not alone.

As the connection with the dragon deepened, I was desensitized by the dragon's strong presence. Then, at some point, we melded, we melded our consciousness. What I have perceived as a being outside of me then became, well, similar to what you call a light body. The dragon was within me and all around me. It was a mutual choice, a choice from the dragon and from me. It's not only that I gave up something, the dragon did also. Because the dragon also made a deep choice for embodied realization on behalf of our common true self, Aouwa.

Still, the dragon would not do anything in my place, he was just there. I, the human part, had to continue to let go. So I did, and at some point when I was in the deepest depths of the void, void of any perceptions, suddenly everything opened up. The final veil lifted. There are no words to describe that. But what appeared to be the void, suddenly cleared up and became the fullness of All-That-Is. All limitations were gone. That tiny, tiny consciousness bubble swimming in what is in reality true creation, suddenly recognized itself for what it really was, "Wow, *I am All-That-Is!*" That was deep. That was not only the communion with true self, that was also a letting go on the level of true self. True self let go of its final, final thin belief in separation.

And when I realized that, the dragon came, nudged me and said, "Hey, listen, Althar, you have to make a choice. You have a body on Earth and you have your realization. What will you choose? Do you want to go back to planet Earth? Or do you want to stay here?"

In that very moment, being absolutely one with Aouwa, my true self, I had the remembrance of the true selves entering into the adventure of incarnation. How they made a promise to each other, "Whoever comes first, will help the others." And that promise rang true to me. I remembered it and, yes, I knew that it would be *very, very* difficult to provide help, for the people in my time, what could I say to them? Could I go back and say, "Well, you are creation, what's the problem?" They didn't even had too much of a problem. They weren't aware of being stuck in separation. They were still exploring the energies while I discovered that there is no energy. Energy is a symptom of separation.

But at that point, the dragon nudged me to peek into my hut in the mountains and see what was going on there. I saw my body lying there on the floor and Echnatara, the young lady who had brought me food throughout all those months, she was sitting next to me. And there was a bond that has been created between the two of us, even from a distance. Echnatara was very special. She wasn't mental in any way, she had no inclination to being scientific, but she was intrigued by what I was doing. I had the feeling that, well, she might be somebody who could be willing to listen or to do the same as I did – go within and experience what it means to be free.

So, in acknowledgement of the promise, not to say the vow Aouwa made and in seeing at least one person that I felt I could be of help for, I decided to go back. I also knew that in essence there's no need to rush. Also, my time was quite different from your time. Back then, there were very few people on planet Earth, so there was only a very thin layer of mass consciousness. Moreover, my community was open to change and I knew I would be welcomed back. Even if I made a very different appearance, they would just be curious. So from that perspective, the choice wasn't too difficult for me. Also, my physical body was quite healthy, I had no ailments, no illnesses. So, it wasn't too much of a stretch for me to return and try to see if I could do anything. Hence, I decided to go back.

I said, we were a bit naive. We had to find out how it works, this high consciousness in the midst of separation. Even though I knew I would be welcomed back in the community, it took me quite a while to adjust to my new condition. So initially I stayed in the hut, Echnatara brought me food. Nothing changed too much. But Echnatara, well, huh, she was a very special one. I felt that she wanted to follow in my footsteps, and I knew that it would make no sense whatsoever to talk to her, because she was of a different nature. She was of an *intuitive* nature. She was of the nature of the heart. She needed to *feel* and *experience* and not to be talked into scientific explanations of what consciousness and thought might be and what happens when you let go.

So what did I do? I just shared my presence with her. I let her feel myself, and I did with her what the dragon had done with me – we were simply together, sharing eye contact and sharing each other's acknowledgement. And that in itself became a strong catalyst for her. I couldn't do it for her, just as nobody can do it for anybody else. She had to make all those choices, but with me being there, she saw, well, there's something more to life, there's a deep, deep change possible. She felt that and she knew that was her way.

After a while, we both went back to the community and took residence in a small temple at the edge of the village. We called the temple "The

Temple of Beauty". It was certainly not a big temple, it was small and cozy in a way. We played there together and, well, in fact, we fell in love. This made my life a bit easier, because everybody felt the change within me and they said, "Oh, he's in love, that's why he has changed." So I didn't have to explain too much.

Anyway, we started our common life there, in the Temple of Beauty. We called it the Temple of Beauty, because beauty was our common thing. We both enjoyed beauty. Echnatara did her own explorations with introspection, with going within in her very own way, and I continued pursuing my passion, namely investigating energies. I intuitively understood there is no such thing as a source of energy. Meanwhile, the dragon has laid out in the books what we came to understand what physical energies are.

However, at some point, I came to the understanding how *intent* and *pure energy* go hand in hand. Then I found out how to anchor an intent in a crystal. You know, intent is the creative impulse and if you are anchoring it in a crystal, you might say, that this creative impulse is modulated, transformed into the physical reality and from there it radiates.

I started out with beauty. Let's see what happens when I infuse beauty into a crystal and let it radiate. So I did. I placed some infused crystals in the temple. The crystals themselves were not particularly beautiful, but whoever came close to the temple or even into the temple, well, they *felt* the radiation of beauty. And suddenly what they were seeing became more beautiful.

I liked it very much. It attracted a few people. I knew at the time I had to proceed very slowly with what I was doing. I wasn't going around and telling people, well, just sit down and see what's going on within you – they weren't ready for that. So I had to go very slowly. I found a few disciples who were kind of ready, who could kind of sense that there was something going on beyond what I was telling.

At some point I noticed, the other communities were getting more hostile. There were kind of wars breaking out. And I felt, hmmh, it might be necessary, if I want others to realize enlightenment, well, not to push, but to create better circumstances.

So I asked myself, "What would be the most helpful intent to embed in crystals?" And I came up with the idea of using *clarity*. You want to become clear about who you truly are and how things work? Well, then you might want to go with clarity. So, I injected clarity into the crystals.

And it worked. It worked very well. But unfortunately not in the way I thought it would work. I said we were a community that was exploring the energies and therefore we had many of – what you would call today – technicians. Those technicians suddenly had clarity. Suddenly, they understood better how the energies worked. They came up with brilliant inventions, new machineries and the new machines even worked. They had no idea *why* they suddenly knew how to apply those energies, they just did it. That's the nature of clarity – you just know and then you do it. And afterwards, you explain to yourself why you knew what you did.

The problem was that these technologies became a threat to the other communities. Words spread. We had an easier life with the new inventions. Every invention, of course, can be misused for martial ambitions. Well, it went well for a time. Still, the word spread, "Something is going in that community. There's a couple living there, they are a bit strange, we don't know what they do – they don't talk too much, they mostly don't talk at all. But whoever comes close notices a change."

Meanwhile, Echnatara continued her own explorations. At some point, she entered into the void, just as I had, and then went beyond. She explained it as feeling an overwhelming sense of a love for self. A love for self that satisfied all needs, literally – not even food was necessary for her anymore. She could sustain herself out of thin air, just as you could.

Echnatara didn't feel obligated to stay incarnated. Her true self, in a way, did not make that promise or vow to be in service to the others. But still she had chosen to stay in her body, because I, Althar, was on a mission and she was not in a rush. So she thought, "If I could be of help, why not? He was of help to me, I will be of help to him. I could leave at any time, whenever I want, going forth into the Third Round of Creation, exploring true creation beyond separation." Thus, Echnatara stayed.

Things developed and at some point some neighboring communities decided, "No, we cannot let that move on, this temple thing is too dangerous for us. We have to intervene. They don't want to tell us their magic tricks, so we rush in and destroy everything." So they waited for me to be back in the mountains for some retreat, because they feared me – I could be a magician or something like that. Then they came. They killed everybody in the whole community and burned it down. The raped the women and killed the children. The Temple of Beauty was destroyed. Of course, Echnatara was tortured, raped, killed, all the rest of that. Oh, she left, she didn't endure that. She felt when they were coming, she knew what was going to happen to her body, so she left.

When she left, she tried to contact me, Althar. Although I was in the mountains I felt it what was going on. I was rushing back. I felt what was going and I knew I would come too late. I could have done something to prevent that, I knew that I could have injected, for instance, confusion into some crystals. I could have hidden the whole community, but I did not do that for whatever reason. So, I knew I failed somehow. Echnatara was trying to reach out to me to come with her, but I said, "No, no, no."

I was rushing back, I was already feeling ashamed, my consciousness was totally collapsing. When I arrived at the Temple of Beauty and saw all the dead bodies, the charred children, be-headed people everywhere, and the dead body of my beloved Echnatara, I totally collapsed. I retreated into my own bubble of consciousness. I closed myself up. I did not want to be seen by anybody. Oh, you might say I was an enlightened being, but enlightened beings playing with separation, uh, they can easily revert. I am the living example of that.

And so I did. I felt a shame that was so strong that I did not want to be seen by anybody. I closed up and I have lived ever since in that small time capsule, in that, well, destroyed Temple of Beauty.

You have to know that the Temple of Beauty was like a portal into the other realms. Me and the dragon, we ventured out from there and did advertising, kind of marketing for incarnation. We said, "See, it *does* work! If I can do it, if others can do it – because I wasn't the first – if others can do it and I can do it then *you* can do it also. So come in great numbers, incarnate, that's the way to go." So, according to my feeling, I have lured many, many entities into incarnation. But then... *this* is the outcome? Looking around in this temple at all those dead bodies, well, I couldn't stand that, so I decided to hide in that time capsule, not to be seen anymore.

What does it mean to be in a time capsule? You relive the same experiences over and over again. You retreat from the broader stream of experiences of the entities and you maintain your own kind of sub-dream, just like you've seen yesterday in the unconscious.

There is a general principle that true selves use. If anybody gets stuck in an incarnation, then there is a kind of "technique" of sending out a fresh incarnation, a fresh portion of consciousness, and give it a certain remembrance of the occurrences of the past. That is what Aouwa did. Aouwa had made a promise to help the others, but I withdrew, I was of no help anymore. So, he had to send out a new string of incarnations. Starting not really from scratch, yet quite fresh, but he had to inject a remembrance of my story, particularly to the one speaking right now, to Joachim, even though he was not the first to be sent out. But he was appointed to bring my story to clarity.

It's a general principle. You come into incarnation – specifically if you are doing your last incarnations – with a certain backpack that is not yours. In a way, you can approach those challenges sitting in your backpack freshly and you might come to a conclusion on behalf of that stuck incarnation from another timeline. And as you do, as you develop that wisdom, that wisdom spreads out. It *could* be picked up by that other stuck lifetime. It could, it doesn't have to, but it could. It's like, "Oh, there's an idea." It's an intuition. You don't know where it came from, but suddenly, it's there. That's the way it works. It's like the intuition I had, "Oh, I have to go within." But where did the intuition come from? Ah, maybe from the future? For how could I have created something like that? It was just there and you shouldn't ask where it comes from, for time is not linear. Suddenly, it's there, you pick it up and you act on it, you claim it for yourself, but in the end, it doesn't matter where it came from. If it frees you – you're done.

So, that's a general principle. How did it work in my case? Well, when Joachim and the dragon... Oh, the dragon, by the way, took on my name after he realized that he could not reach me anymore in my bubble of shame. Echnatara could not reach me and the dragon could not reach me either, because *I* decided to cut myself off from everyone. Even though our consciousness had melded, the dragon remained the dragon. He had his wisdom, had his knowingness of who he is. So, in honor of me, he took on my name, Althar, and departed. That's where the name of the dragon comes from.

When Joachim wrote that first book in your era – actually, as I heard, it went quite fast; just a few days for the first book – when he wrote the final chapter, well, the book was finished, but not the events that occurred within him, for he saw repeatedly a very strange image: a wire model of fallen pillars. Well, it was not *that* detailed, just some lines, but it was nagging at him, it wouldn't go away. At some point, he did ask Althar the dragon, "Althar, what is this?" And he *had* to ask, if he wouldn't have asked, well, the story would have gone differently. But he *did* ask and said, "Bring me there, I want to see what that is."

So, he made a trip with the dragon and you might say they entered my time capsule. When Joachim saw the burned down village, the broken temple, the corpses everywhere, he knew something terrible had gone on here. He recognized the fallen pillars of the temple, and then, behind one of them, he saw me, sitting there in desperation. We had a brief, brief eye contact, very brief.

He saw what appeared to be a crazy man from a long bygone era. But I saw, in a way, my own future. It was a very brief encounter. The dragon and Joachim left. Joachim was a bit disturbed by all of that and couldn't make too much out of it, other than being with it. But I sensed that there was something beyond myself. I started remembering. With this brief encounter, I started remembering my own nature. I, once again, became aware of my awareness and pretty soon, I was able to let go of that bubble of shame.

Now, consciousness is a curious thing. You might think that you have been sitting in this kind of bubble for 50,000 years, whereas in reality, it might just have been for three minutes, or a few heartbeats. You don't really know that when you are in a time capsule and, in essence, it doesn't matter for time is not linear anyway.

So, at some point, I opened up again and released myself after this brief encounter with another human, with another version of myself from the future. When I finally, figuratively speaking, looked out of my bubble to see if the others would throw stones at me or boo me, but nothing like that happened. They all said, "Finally! Finally he did it. You are welcome."

I tell my story for two simple reasons, to make you aware of two things. Even if you are enlightened, you can still fall down, you can fall prey to the stickiness of separation. But in the meantime, we have learned a lot, and even if you might not have conscious remembrances, you have heard a lot about religions, spiritual orders, group dynamics and all the rest of that. You can tap into that knowingness, you have a pretty good understanding of what an enlightened being on Earth should do or should not do. So, anyway, this is one thing I want to convey. Please, please be careful with what you're doing in separation.

The second thing is, at some point, you as a living human have to let go of those packages that were given to you as your supposedly problems that you need to work on in this lifetime. You see, as Joachim had me resonating with him, he had to somehow find a way and, huh, he had to come to the very realization that separation is not real. So this is, in a way, the ultimate wisdom. This is the wisdom that heals everything. But *the same holds for you!* You had that very same realization. And for that very reason, it is time for you to let go of this backpack of what you might call your past lifetimes that are still with you, and, in a way, haunt you unconsciously. Therefore, we will now do a trip.

Yesterday, you have been in your unconscious and you visited the Hall of Your Personal Aspects. Next to that hall is another hall. It's called the Hall of Your Previous Lifetimes, and I invite you to go there with me.

We go straight there. We will play a bit of music to enhance the experience for I really want you to go into your feelings and to allow what is going to happen.

(music plays)

We have sent out a team for each and everyone of you into your personal Hall of Previous Lifetimes, to all of those stuck entities sitting in their time capsules. We gently, gently nudged them and conveyed to them non-verbally, "Hey, you! Listen! You want to be aware, for very soon there will come a bright light, a version of your future. You might be curious to have a look at that one. Just so you know, in case you're interested, be aware."

All of you, please, as you did so often these days, become aware of your light body, your pure consciousness, the bliss. It doesn't take long, you've experienced it and the more often you do it, the faster it can go. Also, we don't have to go through a long tunnel or the vent of a volcano to reach all of your previous lifetimes, no, we are just there at the gate.

Once again, we are entering there as observers. We're entering there to *say good bye,* like the dragon said goodbye to me and just like Echnatara said good bye to me. Both are the most compassionate beings I've ever encountered, but true wisdom sometimes means that you have to go, you have to leave an entity alone, for that is true compassion, to honor *his* chosen experience.

Please, enter into your personal Hall of Previous Lifetimes. *No pity!* Be here as pure consciousness, as the true self of all of these lifetimes. They can feel into your signature, into your true name, because that is what they share with you, that is why they recognize you. This signature radiates into that darkness, into this timeless hall of time capsules. Some of them might come close to you and look you into the eyes. But you know what to do – just be who you are. They could pick up your wisdom or not – that's is not your concern. Take a few minutes here, be very open to what happens. Be the observer.

*

You had many great lifetimes, believe me, for you had to play on all sides of polarity. You created spiritual orders, led armies, were the emperors, the kings and all the rest of that. You were the slaves, the soldiers, and the torturers. You know it all. And so many of those lifetimes did not end that well. In some lifetimes, just like mine, you had the wish to be of true help. You interfered with the others, wanted to help them, to lead them to whatever – glory, enlightenment, god –and you screwed up, just like I did. And they're sitting here, waiting.

If you really had a great lifetime, say you were a pharaoh... You decide, "Well, let's build a big pyramid and a great temple." And then thousands and thousands of people start their work. If you play the role of a god incarnate and you do the rituals, you do the walk amongst the people and they all bow to you... *that feels good, believe me.* Ever after that, in subsequent incarnations, you might feel tiny, for you remember somehow that appreciation, the inner fear and respect from the others. So, what could you do in your next life-time after you had *such* a lifetime? It will most often be just the opposite. You feel belittled, small, for you still remember the greatness that you've enacted.

And here he sits, the dead pharaoh, waiting to be called by his priests to do the next great cere-mony. He's waiting and waiting and waiting, but he's long forgotten. Say goodbye to him. The fi-nal goodbye. It's time for you to move on in true compassion.

There is no reason to rescue anybody here, for you know, this is a dream anyway. *Do not make it real* by going in and pitying any dream figure that you made up.

Wave a final goodbye. You are done with solv-ing the problems of other lifetimes. You might bow to these versions of you, for, in the end, they made you into what you are today. But now it's time to move on. It's time to move on, to leave that hall.

*

(music stops)

Time to close the door once and forever. No need to come back, no need to *ever* come back. No need to heal anything, for yesterday you have seen the very core reason of separation: The believe that separation is real. You are beyond separation. And this wisdom, this highest wisdom, penetrates *all* of you at all times. This highest wisdom is available to all of these past lifetimes, aspects, whatever lifeforms you've ever had. They will pick it up sooner or later. It's not your business anymore. Can you allow it to be that easy?

So, dear friends, what do you intend to do in your fresh, new life without all the baggage from the past and even the baggage from the future? Just one hint: Do not push anything! You cannot know the outcome and separation is sticky.

I love that term: Choose the Eye of Suchness at every moment. I really love that term. If you do that, you cannot go wrong. If you do that, then every deed you do is without agenda, it has no back spin. It is not done to come back to you, to mirror something back to you. That is the way of the walking master, of the embodied ascended being.

You see, the pharaohs, they played a role of being a god incarnate, the son of god and all the rest of that. It felt good, but it wasn't real. Nobody might know you for who you truly are, but *you* know. You are the *true* walking god on planet Earth, you're sovereign, free. You're a conscious visitor in the dream of separation.

Every breath you take will make that transition for all the entities within separation easier. That is the vow fulfilled – those who come first help the others. It's not that they're letting down ropes and pull those others out, it doesn't work that way. You are just here, in your presence, in your compassion, and in your wisdom.

So, with that I gladly hand over my name, Althar, to the dragon for I do not need a name myself. Well, I have a name, huh, with my true self.

Ah, by the way, did you come across your name? Once again, feel into the signature of your true self. You will need it tomorrow, as I have heard.

Who would have thought that my story, apparently a long time later, would lead to something like this. A group of people sitting in a normal living room, no temple, no church, no ashram, nothing special here. *Isn't that wonderful?* You just strip off time – which doesn't exist anyway. Consciousness is a wonderful thing and so is life beyond separation.

So, I bless you. All the best wishes also from Echnatara. We will continue watching you, being with you and, if you so choose, you may come in contact with us. Well, you also have your personal dragon, if you so choose.

I am Althar, the Atlantean. Thank you for listening.

6. Questions and Answers

JOACHIM: So we come to the final session for today. This is estimated to be five hours long, is it okay for you? (chuckles)

We have put on the heating - just in case. (laughter – it was a very hot day) We want to see ashes this time.

Okay. This is just meant to be a casual "be together". If you have anything to share, if you want, or if you have a question, then now is the time for that.

ATTENDEE 1: Can I ask you about the second book? The Magi.

JOACHIM: The New Magi, yes.

ATTENDEE 1: The New Magi. Was it a reference to a biblical magi in that era?

JOACHIM: The biblical magi?

ATTENDEE 1: You know, the three wise men they are called.

JOACHIM: Ah, no, it wasn't. It wasn't.

ATTENDEE 1: I was wondering.

JOACHIM: It was interesting. At first, there was this title and I thought, oh, it's a cool title, and then came all the rest.

ATTENDEE 1: Okay. (laughter)

JOACHIM: Whenever I do something, most often first I need to have the title or the image like, the cover graphics and then... You do the same?

ATTENDEE 2: Yeah.

JOACHIM: (laughing) What do you do?

ATTENDEE 2: I know from writing books, children books. I need to have the title first, and its like a thread, like the beginning of everything.

JOACHIM: Yes. Same with "The Free human" – I thought that's a really great title (laughing). There needs to be a book with that title, so let's do it.

ATTENDEE 3: I have one question. If I understood Althar, the Atlantean, right, he said that we – maybe he didn't say that – but we have this baggage of previous lives, because of the connection to these lives. That's not to process them or anything like that, but just if we are wise enough to gain our wisdom then we can share this wisdom with them, because of this connection.

JOACHIM: It's more general. The way I see it, if you create that wisdom or come to a conclusion for yourself then metaphorically speaking that wisdom spreads out, so to speak, through your true self. And by that it touches those who might be interested in it. So it's not that you have this insight and then you go and feed them your wisdom...

ATTENDEE 3: But why then do we have this baggage?

JOACHIM: Well, first it's kind of an imprint within you. It's just there. I call it baggage, but it's not only that, it's many things. It's turning your attention somewhere, like in my case, into that direction of Atlantis. Five years ago, if I heard talks about Atlantis, I thought, "What? Atlantis? I don't care about this crap. Might have been or might be not have been – it is not my problem."

But slowly, slowly these things came up and they suddenly fit together and I find myself in a set up like this workshop. This guy, the Atlantean, I have felt him so strongly all of my life. And that's interesting, because he wasn't "me", it was not "my" lifetime. I am *this* lifetime, whatever that means, but there's an association with him.

By you being... not imprinted, but being in resonance with something stuck, you naturally gravitate to it and deal with it. In the case of Althar, the Atlantean, I *had* to deal with his point of view, like, "Hmmm, I talked so many into doing this kind of adventure and now they are stuck. How do I get them out?" Like you've built a house and it's nice, it's a skyscraper and everybody goes in, but then you realize, "Oh, I forgot to build a way out." Now they are in there, scratching on the walls, "Ah, how do I get out?" And you feel, maybe you should help to create a way out.

It's just like that. And by you then finding a solution from your new perspective in a new lifetime, where you are not yet stuck, so to speak, then you can have, well, an intuition, an insight, a wisdom created from that, which then spreads out. But that "spreading out" is not your part. You just create the wisdom by solving that problem for yourself – so you think – or for your backpack. And then the, say, Atlantean sitting there or whoever is captured in his time capsule, well, he might pick it up. But that's not your concern.

ATTENDEE 3: I understand that. But I think, actually, he proposed that we should leave these past lives behind.

JOACHIM: Yes, absolutely.

ATTENDEE 3: Not to be connected with them, not to…

JOACHIM: Well, you are connected, in a sense… Continue?

ATTENDEE 3: You can answer.

JOACHIM: The point is, when you come to realize the core reason of all the problems, which is the belief in separation, then you have the one key that solves everything. And with that insight you act from a very different level.

You may have healed your inner child or something like that, and it works. Then your inner child from this lifetime is healed, fine, but all the rest is still there. Some of it might be healed also, in a way, but the inner child is on a very different level.

It's like pruning a tree, "Oh, there is a branch, we prune that or cut it off" but the rest of the tree is still there. But now you go to the very core and you uproot the tree by seeing things as they truly are. And suddenly there is no reason for you to make those remnants of dreams true by pruning it. For if you would do that, with the understanding that you now have, you would go in and pamper your, whatever, aspect who is hanging around, and so you make that occasion "real." You give validity to a dream. This doesn't work. It might work in the dream for that specific entity. Somehow it might make you feel good about that, but this is not your job anymore.

Most often it doesn't even work, for the stuck aspects like what they're doing, just like humans. They like being in their time capsule. If you look closely, well, most humans do exactly that. They're getting older, but they are just repeating the very same things. And if you talk to people who are caring for old people, they say "Oh, they are still reading the newspaper and drinking coffee. That's wonderful." Yeah, that's a great life, isn't it? It's a time capsule, repeating, repeating, repeating and they don't want anything, they want it that way and that's okay. That's also true compassion, to allow them that experience, until exhaustion, until they ask three times. And then you might try to share something.

So, at some point you just have to say. "No!" And I love this story very much, for Echnatara left Althar. She wasn't in his time bubble nurturing him, trying to get him out, trying to convince him, "It's not your fault and you are not responsible for the others." True compassion is sometimes to just move away, for the good thing in separation is, everything fades, even the bad stuff. And that is what happened. And time is very relative, so you cannot even say how long this state occurred to him. He would say it was long, but in reality there's no real measurement.

Same for the dragon. He realized, "I cannot do anything here, so why should I bind myself to him. There are others that I might inspire or support, who are actually asking for it. This one now has chosen to pity himself, so I honor him, but bye, see you soon."

And that's hard. The human doesn't like that. The human always wants to help everybody. (someone laughs) Yeah, and it's not always easy. But the question is really, what is the core reason for a human wanting to help anybody? And so often it is self validation. Giving you some self importance, "Oh, I don't know what my life is all about, so, well, I can at least help the poor children in India or the whales or whoever".

The point is, once you're truly free, you can do all of that *without* any agenda. You can still do it. But then without being attached to the outcome, without feeling pity for anybody. You just do it freely and you do your best, whatever that means. That doesn't mean that you enjoy it totally, but you are not bound by it. You do not need to mirror yourself. And then you can be of *real* help. Then suddenly the guy who is in need of help, the old parent, whoever, suddenly feels, "Oh, there is something more."

That's the way it should be, that's the true help, true compassion. Not neglecting the things that are right before you. Whenever I say this is a dream, it doesn't mean you should just reject the things you see – this is where you are living in. This is where you are bound to for the most part of your time. So, deal with it. Cope with it with wisdom and go from there. And then have the moments of enlightenment and see the whole picture. Over and over again.

This is something that is worth pondering. In the Buddhist terminology you would ask, "How can you act without creating karma?" Action means karma. Karma means action. And whatever you do in reality comes back to you. That's just the way it is. But how can you act without creating any attachment? Well, if you are not attached to the outcome, then there is no backward spin to your actions and thus you can act without creating karma. Because, in a way, you are not even interested in the outcome. Yeah, you glance a bit at it, somehow (chuckles), but not in the way of, "Ha! *I* made it, *I* am the great one who saved the whales." And this is true wisdom practiced in reality.

ATTENDEE 4: That's the only challenge, you know. Because we are all conditioned to cause and effect. We do X to produce Y. We go to school to learn. Everything we do... I was conditioned to a cause and effect life. You want to give up your agenda, you want to allow this and that. But that's the real challenge – to let that go. That's for me where passion is stopping. That's the repetitions we are not even aware of.

JOACHIM: This reminds me of a great Zen story. I forgot the details, but it is exactly about this issue. They were great people, those guys. The story was about karma. A dead fox was found somewhere in some monastery and then the master came and said, the fox was a reincarnation of a great master who had to come back as a fox, because he has *denied* cause and effect. And that's very interesting. You are here in a cause and effect based reality, you should *not* deny the dream when you're *in* the dream, but that doesn't mean it has to affect you. This is a very deep wisdom, and it's quite a challenge to live it. The typical human wants to be, well, the star of polarity. "I know how it works, I surf the circumstances." It might even work for a while, even a whole lifetime. But in the long term, it doesn't work so well. *Seeing things as they are while not denying cause and effect* – that's a deep one. That's a deep one. It's like Althar's story. He didn't deny separation, but he fell once again into it. As a result, you come back as a fox, or you stay in a time capsule – it's more or less the same.

ATTENDEE 4: Yeah, exactly. It's almost like a caution in the end. You free yourself form it and yet in that moment of crisis, we call it. And he was caught in the spin of it again.

JOACHIM: You think you are beyond, but suddenly it gets you – *oops!*

ATTENDEE 4: Yeah, it comes from a different angle.

136

JOACHIM: Yes, and it disguises itself in many ways and forms and that's why one should never assume, "I'm *done!* Noooow I am the enlightened being." Yes, you *are* done, but on a moment by moment basis, as I would say.

ATTENDEES 4: Yes.

JOACHIM: But don't come to me and say, "Tomorrow I'll be done or yesterday I was done." I don't care what was yesterday. (chuckling)

And this principle is not that easy to understand, but I would say in the end this is the greatest relief, for you don't wait for tomorrow anymore. You give your best *now*. You cannot do any more than your best, meaning, well, being as present as you can, without falling into the illusion once again or feeling bad about separation. No, there's no point in doing that.

And actually, you do not really know the entirety of your unconscious. We can do this kind of journeying and make ourselves aware and you can, well, you can tell yourself, "I shut the door." Maybe you did, hopefully you did. But some aspects may creep in again. And then you just remind yourself, "I keep the door shut" or you go in there once again, playfully, and say, "Lie down and puff away!" or whatever, without getting into the details of anything specific.

This is one of the core points with this whole journey into the unconscious. Just become aware of its content, not thinking you have to clean anything. It's just the remnants of dreams and that is the important point to understand. But sometimes it's very, very difficult when it's personal. But, nevertheless, what's the best you can do? You can get enlightened in the now and act from there. Can't get any better.

ATTENDEE 4: Can I ask you about something I thought about Atlantis. There's a lot of stories coming up now about Atlantis. I'm just thinking of the story you just told about Althar and the recent stuff in Crimson Circle. And then I read an interview with Elon Musk and so on of where we're going with AI. And it's like when I read the story in the second book about Atlantis, I just felt – this could be today, this is where we're going today again with technology and with the other communities that didn't have the same awareness. This is just a repetition of an old story.

JOACHIM: Yes. It always was a repetition. Yes, yes.

ATTENDEE 4: Yeah. And okay, we have our roles to bring the consciousness into this development of where we are going, that we can in some way impact – this word I don't like – but in some way have an effect on the development of technology. But is there another thread we can bring to it? And what is going on in pre Atlantis? Is there another thread that can save us – you know, save us is the wrong word as well – but, everything seems to begin in Atlantis, we go back to Atlantis. But we never go back to pre Atlantis.

JOACHIM: Yeah, but for what reason? The point is – *this is a dream.* There have been many,

many, many cultures and realms providing always the same experiences. Atlantis is kind of popular for its downfall. People tend to remember it, Plato wrote about it and all the others hooked in. It doesn't even make a difference at all whether it existed or not, because the principle is always the same: things go up and they fall.

If Atlantis is the first or the 100th culture on Earth that fell just doesn't play any role. Because the *principle* is always the same. Understanding that principle, I would never go as far as to say there is a mission or specific reason why you're here right now. Hmmh, maybe there is, maybe not. The main reason for me is, well, to get out (chuckling) and assist or inspire those who are willing to do the same. And what happens on the large scale, what truly happens is non-linear.

I'd say it would destroy your human mind if you were to delve too deeply into that. Really, there is no outcome from that. You can just do your best and the best is to be as present, as open as you can be in each and every moment. And if that influences somebody else, fine. And all the rest, well, I'd abstain from it. Because it brings you into a different mode. At least, it does for me. "Well, we are all here to give a spin to technology." Maybe, but it wasn't that easy prior to World War II either. Look at what happened there. We could have been there for the very same reason to bypass all this this killing. And if you go further backwards, well, any point in time was like that.

So now, yes, it might be even more severe with people getting more and more detached from their bodies and getting more and more into the mental. And I would agree, it is, in a way... what I feel is, it's not getting easier, but maybe that's because I am aging also. (laughter)

"Oh, the poor kids, they cannot to do it the way we did, and it's getting difficult for them." But still, I see the kids rising up with their non-existing attention span and I wonder, well, can they be still for a moment, can they do that? But actually, I don't know. They have to figure it out by themselves. They will have more examples, hopefully. They have the resources that we didn't have at the time. There was no internet thirty years ago to google Atlantis, there were only some weird books that you had to find somehow. So, who knows what truly goes on.

I have a personal opinion though, but it doesn't influence in any way what I would talk about. My opinion is: It's not getting easier, so you better do it now. Don't postpone. That's the only thing I see.

I would say, after the early nineties there was an uplift in consciousness. We had all this freedom movement in the east and everywhere. We were feeling, "Oh, oh, everything breaks up and consciousness is free and people want to decide for themselves!" No, they don't. The Egyptians have been ruled by emperors and pharaohs and dictators for thousands of years. They don't change overnight just because they could. They just don't, they don't want it, they cannot deal with it. And that's true for so many other nations.

So, it goes always like this. It feels like one step forward and then it feels like two steps back. But these two steps back can be the next impulse to go way beyond or way down. You'll see when it occurs. But in a human timespan, well, it might change tomorrow, but the probability is that in the next ten to fifteen years things will not change drastically for the better. People get more and more weird by the day, if you ask me, and the rulers don't make life any easier. So, do not postpone, this can only be for the better. But don't be attached to any outcome, because then you feel guilty if it just goes on and that doesn't help anybody.

ATTENDEE 5: I read last night between 01:15 and 02:30 so my recollection might be... that's why I ask. But I was really struck, it seems like it's the first time I heard the reason, the root cause reason, of why so many people have self-worth issues. You know, the compression, and that we've done something wrong and guilt. So, again, I know this is probably because of the time I read it, and will reread it. But what's the solution, is it to simply realize that it was just...

JOACHIM: Yeah, the very fact that there is no self in the way that a human, for instance, assumes to be a self... It just doesn't exist. It's a false assumption from the outset. It's an impossible thought, "I separate myself from the whole." It doesn't work. But once you do that – zzzzap –

you are sucked into that thought, and consciousness without time is quite fast. That's the way I like to describe it. *Boom* – everything is suddenly there, because separation is applied to itself. It ends up with fantastic separations, like trees and flowers and piles of cells and whatnot. I called that the ocean of scene spheres that you then dive through, but they all already exist. And they are repetitious, because separation, well, it doesn't have the capacity for true creation. It is impermanent and by that everything fades, including that very core that wants to mirror itself, because it doesn't know what it is. It holds on to separation for the fear of being extinguished. It's like, "I ponder separation. Oops, now I'm in. But if I let go, I would die, so I better continue."

And then at some point in that story, we ended up with recognizing all the creepy things occurring in separation. Then we have replicated the original separation with the compression. You once again forgot all that you are, you got down, down, down into density and became a physical entity, having again forgotten all that you are like in the very beginning. But in physicality, you experience in slow motion. And from there you just let go, you realize – because it's so slow – you suddenly can realize truly form within, "Ah, yes, yes, it's true, separation is just a gimmick." And then – where is the dream.

ATTENDEE 5: So, just by realizing that everything will be…

JOACHIM: Yeah, but not so much on a mental level. I think, it's quite easy to say, "Well, I agree, sounds reasonable, good."

ATTENDEE 5: That's kind of my point. How do you apply that practically to people?

JOACHIM: Yeah, yeah. It's not practical, in a sense, that you go to the bakery and tell the sales guy, "It's all just a dream." "Oh, really? I have to pay my rent tomorrow. So, what do I do now?" "Well, don't know. Just pay."

It's not practical in that sense, but it is the only way out. But you have to realize it on a *deep* level. I think the first step is always to even ponder it. "*Could* that be real? Separation is just a belief?" And then you fight with it. And then, of course, everybody wants to bargain. "Yeah, this is *kind* of true, but I better prepare for the worst." But you cannot bargain with polarity. You just cannot. And this understanding doesn't come easy. It just doesn't come easy, so don't push it or fight it. But at some point, it is undeniable, and *then* it comes from within. *Then* you just surrender. But to *what* do you surrender? To what you truly are. Surrender just means, "Oh, this tiny bubble of separation that brings all this crap up *is not real*." And then you ask yourself, "What was the point? Why did I hold on to it?"

It takes its time, but at some point, it is undeniable. And then it's still to be brought into life, but in a very different way. It's not from the head, because then it's not a theory anymore. That's what it means, "End of preparation." Bring that to experience and from there bring it into real life and embody it. That's a mouthful.

ATTENDEE 5: Yeah, I think that's what I was curious about, if there is something – maybe I had a false impression – but how to assist others in realizing that it is just futile, the guilt. I'll refer them to your books.

JOACHIM: Uh, uh. Right, if it helps. Well, that's the Koan, as you would say in Zen. How to act in daily life? That's the greatest Koan. What do I do now in this given situation? What does true wisdom tell me to do? What is this entity or this group or whoever is there capable of understanding? What is true help? That is so difficult. Sometimes true help is to let them go or let them fall until they come to the very depths and then they might evolve from there. Cuddling them might be the wrong approach or it might be the right, depending on the situation, depending on your situation with them. There is no right or wrong answer, it depends even on your character. Are you more of a heartfelt being, the compassionate one or are you more – don't know – more of the hardcore version? It depends on the situation and on the people involved.

Enough talk for today, yes? Has anybody a final question? A final comment?

ATTENDEES: Thank you.

JOACHIM: Thank you!

7. The Signature of the True Self – Revoking the Hypnosis – Releasing the Blueprints – Opus Magnum

We will start the day with a bit of silence. Take a few minutes to bring in your light body. Become totally aware of your physical body, connect to the level of your true self, have the intent of having a light body, and bring forth the feelings – all on your own.

Take your time. When you are done, we'll have some music and another guest.

(Ten minutes of sitting in silence)

* * *

(Music "The End of the Dream", from *Evanescence*)

(Background music plays)

I am Aouwa! I am the beginning, the end, and the beyond of All-That-Is, and I am an elder of Uru.

Today we have a very special day. It is a celebration. We celebrate the end of the dream. We celebrate the end of preparation, for both of this goes hand in hand. Now it's about bringing it to practice, bringing it to life.

You might feel into our amphitheatre today. There were some changes. Today we have many,

many representatives of the various spiritual families. They are watching you from the non-physical. For you are here as a representative of your very own spiritual family. You are here to find the way out and then to transmit it to your family.

Now, what is a spiritual family?

Feel back into the very, very, very first moments, when consciousness found itself within separation. You didn't know who you were. You felt quite desperate. You suddenly found yourself in a completely new environment, even though there was nothing other than you.

You didn't know who you were, but within that separation you brought forth intents and those intents were mirrored back to you. Those reflections gave you an idea what you *could* be.

You *longed* for stability, for where you came from was, in a way, a "constantness." But now you felt change and you longed for permanence. Of course, at that time you did not "think." But what you did, what all of us did at the time, was to repeat the same intents so we got the same reflections.

Through these repetitions, we all created what I now call the first false identities. We assumed we were those reflections.

By always repeating the same intents and absorbing the reflections, we created a kind of blueprint. A pattern for repetition that we held on to.

Now, consciousness is grand. It is *vast*. It is an ocean of oceans and even if it is bound to express only in separation, it has an *enormous* amount of potentials. Thus, there were so many different ways of starting out into this ocean of consciousness, into this ocean of potentials and the various entities took different routes.

Nobody can say, *why* anybody took on a specific initial pattern of mirroring itself, but in the end this is what led to what you now call spiritual families. Entities that created similar initial patterns bonded with each other, just as you do right now in the human realm. You feel attracted to those who are similar to you. You say, "Here I feel at home. In a way, *they* understand me."

Now we say, you just share the same illusions, that's what a group is. But it served a very good purpose. It was your way to start out. From there, all of those families went out and explored separation. They ventured out, refined their experiences, refined their creations or aggregations, that were formed out of separation. They went into the various densities. Of course, sooner or later they met other families and after some interesting experiences of getting to know each other, there was friction – as always, because we are in separation. From there, we went all the way until we discovered the standstill.

To this day, at the very core of all the true selves are their very blueprints. The blueprints are kind of related to your DNA strands. The DNA is used in biology to create a certain body and define your features. Do you have wings or not? What can you feel? What can you perceive?

But there is much more to the DNA strands, even though you cannot see these features in the physical. So many emotions are imprinted, memories, patterns for bare survival, and patterns for reflecting yourself within yourself. The human DNA is special in that all species that have ever existed throughout the cosmos have brought their physical representation of their blueprints into the DNA of the humans.

That's why you have *so* many different humans. Different in the ways they behave, act, feel, and express. Even though they all look the same, having two arms and two legs. The reason is that, here on Earth, so we all hoped, you would find the resolution for the standstill on behalf of all of existence by letting go of your very DNA and thereby inspire the true selves to let go of their very own blueprints. For you might say letting go of the blueprint on the level of a true self is even more difficult than letting go of the DNA here on planet Earth.

This is what defines the true selves. This is what they hold on to. Yes, the true selves have a certain fear of being extinguished, because they do not know what will happen once they let go of the very thin definition of themselves, of their own notion of self, their own border, their own shell.

In addition, in the very light density on the level of the true selves, things are *so fast*. Things are *so fast,* it is *very* difficult to *really* have an understanding of what you call cause and effect. So even if you, as a true self, come to the realization that there is something like a belief in separation and that the way out might be letting go of that, even if you attempt to do that, there will always remain a residual of doubt within you. You do not really believe yourself, you do not. That's why, in this light density, we only call it the *principle* of ascension.

Yes, it is possible – in principle. And yes, there have been entities on that level who in a way "did it," but they did not do it to the utmost extent. There is a tiny, tiny residual that still ties them to a limited existence. Not in any way limited as much as a human is, but still limited. However, *a god is not limited!* Even though from the perspective of a human such an entity – and even a "normal" true self – has enormous capabilities.

Expressed in your terms, *limitation sucks!* You want to go fully beyond it.

Uru is a family which investigated consciousness from the outset. They researched the "mechanics" of consciousness, trying to understand it. Not in a mechanical way, but in a "consciousness-way." They also tried to find helpful means to let go of illusions, to illuminate illusions. That was *their* quest. That's what bonded them together.

In that sense, Uru as well as their greater family Uriel, never went that deep into the illusions. They did not get that stuck. Well, therefore they lack certain experiences that other families might have had. So there is no better or worse, it's just the way it is. But because they have been a bit reluctant in going so deep into the detailed experiences, they conducted their research without carrying too many illusions and came up with the compression technology and the hypnosis technology.

As we have said yesterday, it was a major milestone being able to recapitulate what really went on when the whole excursion into incarnation started. Right now we can say, yes, the critical mass has been reached. Enough humans of clarity have released or accepted the greater reality of what led to the compression and hypnosis, to all this fear and shame that were imprinted in your very DNA, in the deepest core of your being.

Just by having allowed yourself to go that far that you can become aware of it without judging anybody – not yourself, not your family – you have let go of it in a way. It is still imprinted in you, yes, it might come up and it will come up, but now you know. And because now you know about it, it has lost a lot of its limiting characteristic. So this is indeed monumental.

Yesterday, we did the light body exercise, but we left out one component. Uru hypnotized a portion of your compressed consciousness so that it wanted to connect to matter and eventually would believe that *it is of* matter. Thus, the other portion of the compressed consciousness could come to the belief "I have a body," and even "I *am* a body."

That hypnosis was crucial, for without that hypnosis, you would have left a long time ago, just as we, Uru, did in our experiments. Oh, we did carry out those experiments, we compressed ourselves. But it was too easy to release that, so a bit of doubt remained.

Thus, we needed a total absence of any remembrance and any echo of your true self within you. You needed to be in the very same place as we have been as true selves when we entered separation – a traumatic experience, not knowing where you are, what you are, how you are. Then, being in such a place, you might realize the final letting go in ultra slow-motion in the physical. The hope was that this would then erase all doubts.

As you know, in the meantime we had a number of ascensions, but as you also know, time does not exist on our level. Thus, it is valid to say that we are both at the very start of this process and already beyond the process. All has been done already, the dream has vanished, but at the same "time," we are just at the beginning.

However, *you* are right in the midst of that dream, no matter if it has meanwhile dissolved or not. An entity being in separation believes separation to be real.

Now we are here, for you are doing your final steps. But as we said, it is not about "you," for that "you" that you think you are does not really exist in the way you think it exists. The moment you fully let go, you will understand what I mean, and that's why you need to trust. Here we are building trust, so that you can do the final letting go.

And when you do it, you will be the light post for your spiritual family. You already have the experience of releasing your biological family. By that I do not mean quitting them or running away from them, but becoming aware of all the energy games that are played within that family, of all the patterns that are engrained and imprinted in your DNA and have been passed on from generation to generation. Once you understood that you are not bound to them, that you can let them go, just as you can let pass any thought and any emotion, in that very moment you released your biological family. By doing so, you did a great service to them, even though they might not have understood at the time or even now. But sooner or later, they will realize, "Oh, it is possible to get out of these grander repetitions that I am in."

Still, your biological family is near and dear to you. You were raised by them, you have deep bonds, you have a resonance with them, whether you want it or not. It is much easier to feel your brothers and sisters, or your father and mother than other entities. Even though you might say, "Well, I do not feel related to them so much," but still you are bonded with them. As long as you are aware of this, as long as it does not color your perceptions, there is no problem with this.

The very same holds true for your spiritual family, and believe me: *You had many more experiences with your spiritual family than you*

would ever have had with your biological family!
This means the bond is very deep, so very deep
that you do not even realize it. It is the backdrop
of your whole existence. It colors you. It defines
your core characteristics throughout all of your
experiences.

So you might carry the characteristics I have
mentioned before, like compassion or wisdom,
transmuting fear, or conducting research. Anything is possible. These are within each and everybody and that's why we all appear to be so very
different. This not good or bad, that's just the way
it is.

By you allowing to let go not only of your biological history, but also by becoming aware of
the very fact that the blueprints exist and *that you
could go even beyond them,* you demonstrate to
your spiritual family that this is indeed possible.
Moreover, by doing so you *change* the blueprints.
Specifically you change the blueprints of your
spiritual family.

Do you get the idea?

It's not that anybody goes out there and fum-
bles with some building blocks. Not at all, but you
set the example. You demonstrate that it is possible. You can let go of that and still exist – you
even exist in a way that is so much grander than
any limited being can ever imagine.

When Uru hypnotized you, it was of course
necessary to have a release trigger built-in. Some-

thing was needed that would set you free, for otherwise you would have been stuck for eternity. But that key needed to be hidden. There could be no external force that could release you, other than yourself, because otherwise, all the energy games and power games would have continued.

Thus, it had to be a *very* specific key for each and everyone of you. The best way to hide a key is to hide it in the obvious. And the obvious in this case is of course your true name, you signature, as I like to call it. The feeling, the knowingness of who you truly are. If you radiate it into the hypnotized consciousness, then you will slowly, slowly wake-up your hypnotized consciousness.

An ow we are going to do exactly that.

So I invite you, please, once again become aware, starting on the level of your true self. It's very easy, for you are already there. Then hold the intent of having a light body.

Feel safety.

The light body envelopes all of your physical body. All of your cells, your organs. It envelopes your emotional body and even all of your memories.

Increase the intensity of your awareness of being safe. Do it joyfully for this is a celebration.

Now, add love. Become aware of the feeling of love that is within your light body. It is there in its essence, in its utmost intensity. So open up to it. Allow yourself to become aware of that love.

A love that is not directed to anything, but that is just there. It is a part of you.

Take the dimmer to increase it. To become more aware of that already present love. Your body rejoices.

All the false identities come to peace, for suddenly they are so satisfied. Unconditional love, just so.

Now, add clarity. You know that you know. Now you know. Now you know *why* you are here, why you made this journey. It was truly bold of you who came here and of your true selves which, metaphorically speaking, split off a portion of their consciousness to have it incarnate here. They risked being crippled forever, not knowing the outcome. But now you know. You have seen the end of the dream.

Use your dimmer. Join all those feelings, safety, love, clarity. Rejoice, relax in them. All is good. *All* is *truly good*.

Become aware of beauty, peace, contentness, completion. There are so many fine attributes. *Completion!* Nothing is lacking. You are full and complete. Not only are you safe, not only are you in love – there is no single piece of you missing. You are whole and complete. No need to search for anything.

When was the last time you felt that way?

Now, bring all of that together as we are approaching bliss. Bliss corresponds to your natural state, pure consciousness, your Godself. A Godself is a self that does not need any boundary, limitation, or reflections of itself. That is bliss.

Now, bring that bliss into your physical body as we did yesterday. Because it is such a joy, bring it in through your crown into the center of your physical body, into your belly. From there, let it grow and expand.

Sure, it's a visual. How could bliss be limited? But from the human perspective, it is such a joy to feel it that way. It's the human style of experiencing it. Bring it in as an... well, as an image, but it is also a feeling that is so real, let it grow and then you realize, "Oops, it is unlimited, it has always been that way."

The basis of your true name is this feeling of bliss, because bliss corresponds to your natural state. In a way it can be said that bliss is the same for all true selves, for it is a quality of pure consciousness. But you have had so many experiences in separation that were converted into what you might call wisdom, and they, in a way, color that bliss. They are combined with the bliss.

Even though time does not exist, you have a certain history. Through your experiences, you developed certain qualities. You are not bound to stick to them, but it is just a fact that they exist within the dream. You are not bound by them, you are not defined by them, but in a way, even though it was in a dream, that was *what* you have dreamt. So, the wisdom of all of your experiences combined with the underlying feeling of bliss, with the knowingness of "You know that you know", make up your signature.

You might find a name that you could voice to other humans if you so choose, but deep within you know that no name could ever capture that feeling of "you."

Now let's dive deep, deep, deep into your physical body. We start out by becoming aware of the area between your nose and your upper lip, for there you are very, very sensitive.

When I say, "Be aware of that." you might visualize your consciousness being placed at a spot in that area. Consciousness does not shrink, of course it does not, but it has the ability to focus on that spot and to be totally aware of what is going on there. And that is what we are doing right now.

You feel the air that enters and leaves your nose while you breathe.

Your consciousness is now like a tiny, tiny spot and if you look up from there into the direction of your nose it looks like a gigantic mountain with two holes. And actually, it is. Consciousness has no size. No matter on what scale it chooses to experience, it never shrinks or grows. It just *is*.

So, from this perspective, your nose and your physical body are like a mountain, even like many mountains.

Now, let your consciousness sink into a cell of your skin where you have just placed your consciousness. Let it sink into one cell.

As we have said yesterday, a cell is a fascinating, a *fascinating* creation. No human could ever understand nor build with his linear mind what is going on in any single cell. It preserves its life. You see molecules swirling from left to right and they just know where to go. They are carrying other molecules. Enzymes are built and copied and somehow they are brought to where they are needed. Do you really believe you can *understand* this in a linear way? And then even to organize this walking pile of cells which constitutes your physical body? This is non-linear, this is the grandiosity of consciousness, even if it expresses itself in separation.

Let's go forth to the core of your cell. Just enter into it and you will find the DNA strands. They are wound up, like twisted rope ladders. Choose one of those strands and become even smaller. Become the size of an atom and glide along a strand. See the life that is going on here, the communication. It's like a firework, a constant firework that is emitted here. This is how these strands communicate. But then, is there any center directing all of this? No, there is not.

Now, come to a halt and choose a single atom of your DNA strand. Visualize it as a sphere, a cloud of electrons swirling around it. You even go deeper towards the core of this atom. Here you can visualize the neutrons and protons as small spheres clinging together with enormous, enormous, enormous energy.

You might say there is a thin layer around these particles consisting of your consciousness. It clings to those particles with the same force as those particles cling to each other. That is the result of the hypnosis. You *wanted* to cling, to attach, to bond on this level, and so you did, because hypnosis is powerful as you know.

Now, here you are. In a way you see yourself. You see the hypnotized part of yourself, the sleeping part of yourself, dreaming a dream of "I am matter. I am matter." which allowed you to join with this physical body.

You do not want to rip this sleeping part of you out of its sleep. Why would you? If there is a child sleeping in its crib and it's time to wake up, you do not go there and shake it brutally. You do it gently, for it might be having a dream, and there is no need to scare anybody or anything that is dreaming. So, instead of shaking this consciousness and yelling, "Wake up!" you simply send your signature towards these particles and your consciousness that is bound to them. You might join your own internal humming of your signature, a multidimensional humming, with the music that is playing. Just add your humming to the music and feel into that. Gently, gently, gently waking up the consciousness that is bound to a single atom. This is how embodied ascension will start – *with a single atom.* Never think an atom is small or insignificant.

You might feel how that hypnotized consciousness is slowly coming into resonance with you. Gently. In a way, it is waking up from its sleep, it's rubbing its eyes, it doesn't really know what happened. "When did I fall asleep? A moment ago? Eons ago?" Oh, it doesn't know. It's dizzy and dazed, but it recognizes *itself,* its own signature which is *you,* being here in awareness. Like a loving mother holding her child. The child recognizes the mother as its mother. So, it knows it is safe and then the magic will unfold.

The magic is that the consciousness that has bound you for so long to the physical now becomes the link between what you call the light body and the physical body. That is actually how the light body becomes partly light and partly matter. That is the way, allowing you to retain your physical body on Earth, to interact with others, showing them a human image, a fully functional body. No need to come in as an ethereal being without a physical form. No, you'll be fully present in the physical, yet you *know* that you come from beyond the dream.

It starts with a single atom.

Now use the dimmer. Increase your signature a little bit, but with that you have to be *really* cautious. Here you need all the wisdom and discernment that you have learned in all those years of your preparation. Don't rush, don't push.

If there would be any need for you to leave the physical, like Echnatara did, you could just go "full volume" with your signature. The consciousness would wake up instantly, because it's the trigger key, and you could leave your physical body. Your physical body would survive, because it is made for survival, but you would have left. Isn't it good to know that you have a way out at any time, if you so choose? And there is nothing you have to *do*. You just apply your name and be home.

But I assume that this is not what you are choosing right now, so you need to go slowly and allow the changes to unfold within your body.

I, as an elder of Uru, ask you *not* to try to do anything actively on this level. This is way beyond the human mind. This is not your task. You will be fully occupied in dealing with the effects of this epochal change within you. You want to *live*, you want to *experience* life, you do not want to bother with what is going on at the subatomic level. It is again Uru and others who will assist as good as they can in this process. It will unfold naturally, but still, there is support that can be given. But this is *not* your concern. You just surrender to yourself, for you know *beyond* time that you *have* already ascended, even though the unfolding *in* linear time is not yet realized. The "how" is not your concern. *It should not be your concern!*

This is magnificent! It hasn't been done very often. It is not an instant change and it even requires experience. As you are amongst the first ones to go through this, you are once again volunteering to provide that experience. If you do not want to do that then, well, then just skip this step with applying your signature. Remain bonded to the physical, do all the rest, make your life easier with the light body exercise, until you feel now is the time for you.

When you have increased the intensity of the signature you are radiating, you might feel it spreading out through the atoms. It spreads out! There is nothing you have to do, it's natural. It's resonance. It's always resonance, isn't it?

This way, slowly, slowly all of the hypnotized consciousness will wake up from its dream in the appropriate time. When it does, it immediately knows where it is and what to "do" for your consciousness is there.

It's a wonderful process and you'll experience it only once, so really enjoy it. Feel the joy of the reconnection within yourself on the deepest, deepest level. It can be said metaphorically, that the hypnotized part of your consciousness was split-off, for it was so "far" away. It was the rubber band that always pulled you back when you went out too far into bliss-mode and bliss-land. *It pulled you back,* because it was chained to the body and wanted to survive.

Letting go of the DNA resembles letting go of the blueprints. And this is the example you set. So, while your are doing it on the level that we have just talked about, you are doing it as well on levels of your consciousness for which we have no words. There you are bound to the blueprints of your greater existence, and it happens there as well.

Now, we'll leave the atom we have just visited and we will slowly, slowly change the scale of what we are aware of. So come back to the core of the cell. From there, feel the whole cell. Come back to the cell on your skin. Become once again aware of your whole body.

Changing the scale of awareness is really not difficult once consciousness has freed itself from limitations, is it? And because it is not difficult, I invite you to get even grander. Expand! Or better said, become aware of your expansion. Become so huge that all of Earth is contained within your light body. All of Earth.

See Earth from outer space. Isn't she beautiful? Yes, harsh at times, but this is *the* spot where embodied ascension is realized. You have put so much love into this place, so much hope, so much dreaming – and now we have come to the end of the dream in each and every aspect.

Now, get even larger. Get so large that you contain all of your solar system. For a normal human, this is huge, but it's nothing for you. There is not much of a difference, being on the top of an atom or containing your whole solar system. Consciousness can do that.

While you are at it, there is no reason to limit you in any way. Just become aware of your expansion and contain all of your physical universe within you.

I love to ask this question: "If there is no separation, where does the inside end and the outside begin?" Does it end at the end of your universe, if any exists?

How could it end there? How could it?

So, why not just go beyond your universe? Become larger. Just do it. Thousand times the size of your physical universe – however large that is. Just feel that and look around.

Not surprisingly, you can see many universes. Each of them is like a tiny bubble, full of separation, full or experiences. They have various characteristics, but always the same taste, the taste of repetition.

Become even larger. Within you, you hold all of the realms that exist, all the physical realms and all the non-physical realms. Now, please, even though you are so large, imagine all these realms to be contained within a single sphere and you are the surface of that sphere looking within.

You are each and every point of the surface looking within. This is called *introspection*. This is the very same thing that you did during the initial ten minutes of this session. You looked within. The scale doesn't matter too much. It's only a question of what you are limiting yourself to. To a human body? To a particle? Or even to all of separation? For it can be said that within the bubble you are looking into right now, *all* of the

Second Round of Creation, all of creation that is based on separation, is contained. *It is all within you.* It's just there.

Separation is a thought that you ponder in every possible way.

Now, let's do an experiment, even though it's a paradox. Instead of looking within from the surface of the bubble, look into the other direction and be surprised what you feel and see, or better said, *know.*

Apply the Eye of Suchness. What you see here is the Third Round of Creation. From this perspective, separation is really a tiny bubble, a thought that is crazy from the outset. An *impossible* thought, and in that respect, it was instantly dismissed. Yes, while you realized that the thought is impossible, many things happened "inside" that thought.

But here is the Third Round of Creation which means here is *no* separation. It means, here is *true creation.* A creation brought forth as a natural expression without limitation. Thus, I say it's an *ever expanding perfection.* It is not static, but it is also not impermanent in the way that you know from separation.

If here is beauty, it is in *ever expanding* beauty. In *ever expanding* beauty, not rising and falling. No.

Just *feel* that, do not analyze it with the residuals of your logical mind.

Sometimes it is said that Nirvana and Samsara are the same, or in our terminology, the Third Round of Creation and separation are the same. The philosophers can argue that back and forth, but from your current perspective you might see that this is a very limited view. I would suggest not to think in those terms, for you might come to the belief that separation is all there is. You might feel unlimited, yet still be in separation – which is possible, by the way – but if you see the whole picture, if you see or feel the Third Round of Creation, then you might see that Samsara is just a tiny, tiny spot within it. It is insignificant. Nirvana and Samsara are not two sides of the same coin.

This is the end of the preparation. This is a celebration that has been awaited for a long time. This is a dream that has been fulfilled.

Isn't it funny? Every dream a creator being dreams will be fulfilled, for that is the nature of a creator being.

Now, here we are once again. In a way, you are all sitting together as you did when you left to incarnate. This is very similar. In a way, you made it, you set the example, you are changing the blueprints with your choices in each and every moment, and the question comes up, "Do you really want to go back and maintain a physical body?"

There is truly no pressure to do anything. Absolutely not, for it can be said that the dream of separation is already over anyway.

On the other hand, those who are still within the dream that is already over, struggle quite a bit. As you know, you had many helpers along your way. Not only all of your ancestors, but also all the wise guys.

So, maintaining your physical body on planet Earth is maybe the greatest gift you could give to all of existence. And it's not a question of "How long?" but it's a question of moment by moment.

And even though I am aware of the Third Round of Creation, I once again state that the beauty you see when an entity within separation opens up to this magnificence... witnessing such a moment is unparalleled.

Isn't it strange that by doing *nothing*, by just *becoming aware of what already is,* you realize what is called the Opus Magnum?

Who would have thought, while being in a human body chasing for outside experiences? It is all within. It always was.

A final remark for all of you. Separation is over for you – you have come to understand that. And even though sometimes it makes sense to take on certain perspectives, like the absolute, true self, the relative, the human, or the mystery in-between, what you might call the dragon, even though it sometimes might make sense to take on a certain perspective, you within yourself should let go of any kind of mental separation between these three. They never existed in the first place, not in reality, and you should become more and more... what's the right term... You should allow more and more the "all of you" being everywhere, even in physicality. It is the living God, the living light, the living trinity that you are. But a trinity that has no separation in any way.

Get used to that truth. No need to limit you any more. But there's also no need to seek for confirmation on the outside. For if you do, it just shows that you have doubts and then you are back in the game of separation. *You do not want that!* Not on this level.

So just *know that you know!*

Be in the completeness that you are.

And be aware that there are other beings around you. Therefore, I invite you once again to *feel* the others that are with you. Don't ask, "How could that be? Everybody is the Second Round of Creation in totality and still there are others?" Well, that's just the way it is. Just as you will never understand a single cell, your human mind will never understand this characteristic of consciousness. But right now you can *feel* it, can't you? Maybe that suffices.

Feel the others for they are with you. They have a human body right now and they're sitting next to you. Others will join you and you will notice each other, you will recognize each other – just as you did when you met each other for the first time here at this gathering only two days ago. Seems like eons ago, doesn't it?

This is the bridgehead in the Third Round of Creation that we spoke of. The synergy of having many humans doing it at the same time makes it easier for all of you.

You might see the spiritual families – they are in delight. *Now they understand.* So many beings of them have never been incarnated, but now they get the idea. They now become aware of what is possible and isn't that always the first step?

So I, Aouwa, thank you for all that you did, not only in these last few days, but throughout all of your lifetimes, for being part of this adventure, for taking the risk, for changing All-That-Is without *doing* anything.

You might say the amphitheatre is now dissolving and that might become a problem for you in the next few days when you are back home, but... you know it all. If sad feelings come up, because this gathering is over, just choose the Eye of Suchness, do not fight the feelings. Feelings and emotions in separation will pass. No need to do anything.

Remember this one choice you have when you fall back into the human condition. The one choice of importance is to *choose the Eye of Suchness*. It is *only* about the current moment. It is in the now-moment that you realize enlightenment, that you realize embodied ascension, and that you realize true love.

I am Aouwa. It was a great honor to be with you for so, so, long.

Made in the USA
Middletown, DE
18 June 2020